Football, Politics, and $13 Billion

by

Coach Billy O'Brien

To a Hokie from a Tar Heel

Billy O'Brien

look at page 48 and 91

RoseDog 🐾 Books

PITTSBURGH, PENNSYLVANIA 15222

The contents of this work including, but not limited to, the accuracy of events, people, and places depicted; opinions expressed; permission to use previously published materials included; and any advice given or actions advocated are solely the responsibility of the author, who assumes all liability for said work and indemnifies the publisher against any claims stemming from publication of the work.

For additional information or to order additional books,
please write:
RoseDog Publishing
701 Smithfield Street
Pittsburgh, Pennsylvania 15222
U.S.A.
1-800-834-1803
Or visit our web site and on-line bookstore at
www.rosedogbookstore.com

CONTENTS

PROLOGUE

In 1984 I was fifty-five years old, and I was five years into my eight-year campaign to bring the lottery to Virginia. I had been fighting opposition from church groups, former governors, the current governor, and almost everyone from the conservative southwestern part of the state. The speaker of the House, A.L. Philpott, was totally opposed to the lottery. I had introduced a bill to have a state referendum on the lottery, and he, in order to make sure that it did not pass, buried it in three committees. I couldn't even get it out of one.

What could I do to bring the lottery to Virginia? And why was I so determined to do so?

All my life I'd wanted to improve teachers' salaries. My first job, after leaving the Marine Corps as a first lieutenant in 1954, was teaching high school government for the enormous sum of $2,900 a year. I'd wanted to be a teacher and coach since I was in high school, and it was very disappointing to find out that my salary wasn't enough to make ends meet. I was married and had an infant son, and my wife had to work, too. I wanted teachers' salaries to reflect their true worth and valuable contribution to Virginia and the nation. I wanted them to be paid well enough to support a family. Billions of dollars in lottery money *could make that possible.*

As a member of the House of Delegates, I knew that there was no way I could carry the House and Senate. I sought a state referendum because I wanted to let the people decide.

In 1984 I came up with a strategy to boost interest in my cause. I started writing letters to all of the editors of the newspapers in Virginia. As a teacher for thirty years, a winning coach for twenty years, and a member of the House of Delegates for ten years, I knew the editors would publish my letters.

In my letters I stated that Virginia had produced great leaders such as Madison, Monroe, and Jefferson, who believed that ordinary people could express good judgment on matters of public concern if given the opportunity to do so. Not allowing the citizens to express their good judgment was an example of elitist paternalism by the elected members of the general assembly.

This immediately caused a lot of publicity. People began writing letters to the editors. Articles were written, pro and con. I had succeeded in bringing the debate for a referendum to the people. The opposition, realizing that public sentiment was changing, began devising a new strategy for defeating the lottery.

Soon everybody wanted to debate me, including conservative politicians and anybody who wanted to get on TV. They thought they could beat me because I'd only been a football coach. I had not done much public speaking, but I was a great speaker in the locker room and I could hold people's attention. I had the facts and believed in my cause.

The letters I sent out and the debates that followed turned the tide in my struggle. My fight would eventually cost me my job as a teacher. It would take some careful strategy and a lot of hard work. I still had three long years to go before victory, but I knew I was getting there when the debate reached the people.

My Early Childhood in Kansas

My father struggled from job to job. He had served in World War I on a destroyer and was trained as a machinist, but work was scarce during the Great Depression. We were poor, but I didn't really know that as a kid. I was born in Parsons, Kansas, on April 20, 1929. My mother was Teresa (Tess) Conway O'Brien. We moved to Chicago briefly, then settled on a small farm near McCune, Kansas.

My father didn't have a job, but we did have a cow, chickens, a large vegetable garden, and rabbit traps. My mother baked bread, churned butter, and made cottage cheese, hanging curds of milk in a cloth bag on the clothesline. We kept milk cold on a rope in the well and also made Jell-O in the well.

We had the best meals you can imagine because my mother knew how to make almost anything taste good. I remember very clearly going with her to gather jackrabbits out of traps. She carried a small hatchet and chopped the rabbits' heads right off. I wasn't real happy about it, but those rabbits sure tasted good when my mother cooked them.

Even now, in my seventies, I enjoy cooking. When I cook, it takes me back to the warm kitchens of my childhood where my mother created wonderful meals. Some of my favorite foods from that time include potato soup with egg noodles, navy bean soup with ham hocks, and French toast. When we'd have French toast, my mother made our own sugar syrup by mixing sugar and water and cooking it down on the stove. My mother skillet-fried squirrel and rabbit on the wood stove. The main things that my parents bought at the country store were flour, sugar, salt, and coffee.

There was a little town about three miles from our house. My father always carried his shotgun when he walked to town. One day we had company coming and we went to the store to get something to feed them. We saw a covey of quail sitting on the ground. My father raised his shotgun and killed thirteen in one shot. "We don't have to go to the store now," he said.

To catch fish, we had a trout line in a stream with dough balls on hooks for bait. My mother made great fried catfish. Every Sunday we always had a baked chicken. We didn't like to kill the chickens because they laid eggs. We had all the eggs we could possibly want and plenty of milk to drink. We never went hungry.

We took our lunches to school. My mother would make chicken sandwiches from the baked chicken left over from Sunday dinner. At school I would trade the chicken sandwiches for peanut butter and jelly sandwiches because we didn't have peanut butter at home and it tasted good. Other kids were glad to get those chicken sandwiches.

I still cook some of those foods. My son and daughter ate a lot of potato soup with egg noodles when they were growing up.

During the time we lived in Kansas, President Roosevelt instituted the Works Progress Administration (WPA). My father was hired to work for a dollar a day repairing roads. At the time many people, including my father and mother, thought that Franklin Roosevelt was the greatest man who had ever walked on the face of the Earth.

My father never had much to do with me. He was close to my mother but not his children. My mother took care of my sister, Eileen, and me. She only went to school through the eighth grade, but she had been the best speller in her school.

Our family got a set of junior classics, stories about King Arthur and the Knights of the Round Table. I think my mother bought them. Every night she would read to my sister and me under a coal oil lamp. One book was all about Sir Lancelot and Camelot. I formed a lot of ideals from listening to those stories about the Knights of the Round Table.

Aside from weeding the garden in the summer, my main chore as a child was bringing in kindling and bigger pieces of wood for the stove. One wood-burning stove in the house took care of all of our heating and cooking. In the winter, we'd heat big rocks on the stove and cover them with cloth or towels and put them in our beds to keep warm at night.

When I started the first grade, we didn't have school buses. People picked up the children in cars. McCune County School was a consolidated school, which was bigger than the one-room schoolhouses common in rural areas then. I've forgotten many of my teachers, but I remember my first grade teacher, Miss Hankins. I still love her. She and my mom taught me to read.

PORTSMOUTH YEARS

We moved to Portsmouth, Virginia, in 1936 when I was seven years old. My father was a machinist and got a job re-sleeving fourteen- and sixteen-inch guns from cruisers and battleships. We hadn't gone to war yet, but the government was preparing for it.

We bought a refrigerator with a big freezer top on it. We could make ice cream in it. I had never even seen a refrigerator before. We also had our first indoor toilet. We got a radio when we moved to Portsmouth, and my mother and father would listen to Roosevelt's fireside chats.

I got to go to the movies for the first time in my life. It only cost a nickel. That was in 1938 and I was nine years old. I would take my sister, Eileen, with me to the movies on Saturday mornings. We would stay and see the same film three times in a row. Our favorites were Hopalong Cassidy and Roy Rogers.

Portsmouth had a population of about thirty thousand. It was the home of the Norfolk Naval Shipyard, which was actually located in Portsmouth. That's where they built and repaired Navy ships. The town was full of sailors. After we went to war, everybody liked the servicemen, but when my family first moved there, people didn't.

Portsmouth had a recreation department, and I started playing football, basketball, and baseball when I was eight years old. My friends were Leo Walsh, Russell Borjes, Rhae Adams, and George Pendergraft. Playing sports was pretty much all we did We didn't have money for anything else.

When I went to Woodrow Wilson High School, the teachers didn't care if students went to school or not. If you weren't there, they just failed you. I failed everything during my first year in high school because I was never there. I skipped school for fifty-eight days with Cat Claw Creecy and Common Carol Myers, a guy known for cussing a lot. We would get on a ferry and go from Portsmouth to Norfolk. Often we would hide in the back of a truck and go wherever the truck went and then hitchhiked back to Norfolk. We had to be sure to have a nickel to get back on the ferry.

Buddy Owens and Colley Owens coached football in the community league. A man who became the long-time mayor of Portsmouth, Irvin

Smith, coached football, baseball, and basketball. These coaches influenced my life, but not as much as my high school coaches.

It was during my sophomore year in high school that I met three great coaches. Together, they were the single greatest influence on my life. Of the three, probably the most important was Dick Esleeck, the football coach. Phess Woodson was the basketball coach, and Howard Mast was my track coach.

These coaches helped build my character. They looked after players. There were tough but very personable. They checked on our grades, our conduct in class, and made sure we were doing well. I started studying seriously for the first time in my life.

During my sophomore year I was playing football in the community league and Irvin Smith said, "Why don't you go out for the high school team?" I was enjoying playing in that league but decided, *why not give it a try?*

It was the first day of practice, and I tackled a guy, almost biting off my tongue. I left my uniform there and went to Coach Smith and said, "I want to come back to the community league." His reply was, "Go back out there. You can make the team."

I did go back and played third-team center on the football team in my sophomore year. I admired the coaches and knew that they had turned my life around. Because of their influence, it was then I decided that I wanted to be a coach and teacher. The coaches told me that a football scholarship might be in my future. That is when I started studying hard.

I spent my remaining three years in high school making sure I did not get kicked off the team. Dick Esleeck was tough. You said "Yes sir" and "No sir" and never "Huh?" Later as a coach I told my players, "Don't you ever 'huh' me." Coach Esleeck kicked nine guys off of the team for drinking on the boat coming back from a game in Arlington. He would boot a player off the team no matter how good he was. I was determined that I would do nothing to cause my dismissal from the team.

My sophomore year I played junior varsity basketball and ran track. On the last meet of the track season against Petersburg High School, I came in second in the shot put and third in the high jump. To get a letter, a player needed five points. Needing one more point, I went up to Coach Mast and said, "How about letting me run in the 880?" He replied, "You've never run in the 880." I said, "No, but I've been running all my life." He said "Go on in there."

That race was mine. I didn't care about the team as much as getting a varsity letter. Without that letter, you couldn't get a date with a good-looking girl. I won the race, and my mother bought a blue sweater and put on that big gold W. I wore it all the time and was even wearing it in ninety-degree weather in May and June.

Only later, after becoming a coach, did I realize the significance of that 880 race. The coaches were thinking, *Hey, that guy is a competitor.*

The next year, my junior year, being on third team was history. I was first-team center on the first day of practice. We had a winning season and almost beat Granby, who had won twenty-nine straight games before they played us. They beat us 7–0.

Under the direction of Coach Esleeck, we won the state football championship in 1947 for the first time since 1926. We had huge crowds for the games. Sports were the best show in town.

Our coaches inspired us to win the state championship. We were playing on a bright, sunny day in Crabber Stadium to a crowd of thirty thousand fans. Hampton scored thirteen points in the first half by using the pass. Our team was stunned. We hadn't had anyone score against us in our first eight games.

The pep talk in the locker room at halftime was memorable. Doctor Cox, our team doctor, said, "My son was in the U.S. Army fighting Adolf Hitler's Army. He was killed by machine gun fire in 1944. You know, he graduated from Wilson High School, and I know he's watching this game in heaven. He's up there rooting for this team, and I know it would make him so happy to see this team bring home a state championship for the people of Portsmouth. Please do this old father a favor and win this game for my son, who helped defend the United States from Adolf Hitler."

After that, Coach Esleeck stood up, with tears running down his cheeks. He said, "I'd rather be dead five minutes after the game than have to walk across the field and tell Suey Eason that he has better football players and that he's a better coach than I am. I'd rather be dead!"

We tore out of that locker room, not to play but to wage war against Hampton. In the fourth quarter, Howard Borum scored our first touchdown and Billy Farris kicked the extra point. They led thirteen to seven. In the next series, Hampton was moving down field and I intercepted a pass from Dick Carneal and took it down field to about their thirty-yard line. We moved the ball quickly with two minutes to play. Billy Farris scored.

Time was running out. The crowd was roaring. All we needed was the extra point. There was a commotion in the stands as former football player Scotchy Hollewell moved toward the field. His nickname indicated his beverage of choice, and he'd obviously been partaking heavily. He walked out in civilian clothes and acted like he was prepared to kick the extra point to ensure our victory. The police had to be brought in to remove him from field.

Billy Farris kicked that extra point and we went ahead. We even scored one more touchdown and won by 20–13. This ensured that we would win the state championship, since our last game was against a very weak team. When we won the state championship, there was a celebration downtown like I'd never seen in my life.

I made All-State and All-Southern and honorable mention All-American in football. After that season I had many opportunities to attend college. General

Robert Neyland, wearing his uniform, came to my house in a staff car and knocked on my door. He was the head coach at the University of Tennessee. My mother said, "Billy, a general wants to see you." I was a bit afraid of him.

To induce me to play for Tennessee, I went to the University in Knoxville, Tennessee, three times. The coaches even got me a date with Annas Acuff. I took her to the movies. Her father was the country western musician, Roy Acuff. I almost went to Tennessee, but fortunately Dr. John McCoy, president of the University of North Carolina Alumni Association, called and asked me if I would like to go to the University of North Carolina at Chapel Hill and take a look at the campus.

I went down to Chapel Hill on a Trailways bus. They had me run races and timed me. I had to take a mental aptitude test. There were no SATs at that time. On Sunday afternoon Coach Carl Snavely called me into his office and said, "We would like to sign you."

"Where are the papers?" I'd seen the town and liked the area. Coach Snavely was a winning coach.

Dave Pond, who made All-State on our football team, went to University of Tennessee and hurt his knee. They sent him home after three months. Tennessee brought in sixty players on scholarship that year and just kept the ones they thought could play first team and sent the remaining ones home. At Chapel Hill they cared about their athletes.

A coach can help people live better lives. The three men who were my coaches in high school were the greatest influences on my life—beyond anything else that ever happened to me. I had a full scholarship to a great university, and they were a big part of making that possible.

GOING TO THE
UNIVERSITY OF NORTH CAROLINA

In September 1948 I packed up a big old trunk and put everything I owned in it and took a Trailways bus to Chapel Hill. I arrived a week before classes started. There was nobody on the campus. The varsity was practicing and they were all staying in one dorm, Mangrum.

I went to Woolen Gymnasium to the Athletic Department and said, "I came down a little early." They told me that I could stay in the dorm with the varsity team. I got to eat at the training table. They had T-bone steaks, baked potatoes, and salad. They thought that was good for you. I didn't even like steak and asked, "When are they going to have some corned beef hash, spaghetti, or hamburgers?"

They had two-a-day practices. Those are killers. At night the varsity players had poker games going in their rooms and were smoking cigarettes and drinking beer. I asked Haywood Fowle, a member of the football team who had shown me around the dorm, "What happens when a coach comes by?" He said, "The coach doesn't come by here." That's because the players were all veterans of World War II and were in their early twenties. That was a real eye opener.

At that time, most guys on teams played for glory and for scholarships. The veterans were there on the GI bill, so they were playing for glory. Some went on to careers as professional players or coaches, but in that era, professional football players didn't even earn enough to live on. They usually had to have a second job to support themselves.

I didn't expect to earn a living as a professional player, but I did hope that by being an all-star player in high school, I could keep my scholarship and achieve the kind of pride and status I'd felt when I wore that varsity letter sweater in Portsmouth, even in ninety-degree weather.

Coach Snavely was a successful coach. His Chapel Hill teams went to a bowl game in '46, '47, '48, and '49. Great players included Charlie Justice, a tailback, who was All-American and went on to play with the Redskins. Art Weiner was an All-American end and caught a record number of passes in his first year as a pro. His professional career ended because he severely injured his knee. He was teaching physical education in a small town in North Carolina and hurt himself during a game with students.

Just about all I did in college for three years was practice football. We practiced six weeks in the winter quarter, even when it was snowing or raining. In the spring we practiced five days a week for six weeks with a filmed scrimmage each Saturday.

The series of practices ended with a blue-white game. The Athletic Department gave the proceeds from the gate to the Monogram Club. The officers of the club spent all this money to take all the members, who earned a letter in any sport, to Carolina Beach for three days. What a trip. That's where I learned the Shag, a Carolina dance step.

We had a winning season when I was on the freshman team as a defensive end. We won all six games. My sophomore year I started the first four games on the varsity team as the defensive left end. We won all of these games, but in the fourth against the University of Georgia, I experienced the worse incident in all of my football career.

My life changed due to my encounter with a running back named Zippy Morocco. He played for Georgia and was so fast that he ran through me, around me, and over me. After they looked at the films of the game, I was demoted to fifth-team offensive right end and was kicked off of the training table.

When I looked at the bulletin board in the dressing room and saw my new place on the team, I started crying. I couldn't accept being around the players after being demoted from first team.

I went to my room, packed my bags, and went back to Portsmouth. The first thing I did was go to the pool hall. Back in those days all the athletes hung out in Rabbit Bland's Pool Hall right in downtown Portsmouth. It had about ten tables and looked like the pool hall in the movie *The Hustler* with Jackie Gleason and Paul Newman.

It was a hot day in September. I'd just gotten off the bus and was hoping to find a cool place to calm down and possibly get some sympathy for my decision to leave Chapel Hill. In the pool hall I saw Harry Hook Hillman, a sports writer for *The Virginian-Pilot*. He was standing in the shadows, not even playing pool. He was a short, pudgy guy who wore thick glasses. Even though he wore a coat and tie, he wasn't a slick dresser by any means. Every athlete knew him. We were all very friendly with him because we wanted him to write good things about us. I walked up to him feeling pretty bad that I wasn't going to be playing for Carolina any longer.

He stared at me and asked angrily, "What the hell are you doing at home?"

I said, "I quit and I'm going to play with Coach Esleeck at the University of Richmond." Coach Esleeck had been my high school coach, and, after winning the state championship in 1947, he'd become the head coach up at the university. He only lasted two years because he couldn't recruit. At that point he was like a surrogate father to me.

Hillman said, "Get your ass back to Chapel Hill and get an education. That's what counts."

I went back the next day. I don't think they even missed me. Some of the players had told the coach I was sick.

Everyone has turning points in life. That demotion from first team shook me up badly and made me reassess my priorities. That's when I decided that I was going to make sure I graduated. Sports would be secondary to getting a good education. I knew that I couldn't coach unless I had an education. My goal from then on wasn't to be a football star; it was to be a graduate of UNC.

Despite that change, I gained a lot from my years on the team. I learned a lot that served me well as a coach. For example, Coach Snavely brought in experts from professional teams for short-term training during spring practice. Dante Lavelli and Mack Speedy were wide receivers for the Cleveland Browns when Otto Graham was the quarterback. He's the one who made the Cleveland Browns the dominant team in the years before the Super Bowl. They taught me how to run pass routes just like the pros did. We did square outs. We did z-in and z-out. Hook passes. Out and up. I could run those just like the pros did. It was really fun working with two pro wide receivers.

In my entire coaching career, my players ran the best pass routes in the state of Virginia. We had some players like you wouldn't believe. One end I coached, Ken Barefoot, played under Vince Lombardi at the Redskins. He even told me later that I was a better coach than Lombardi, but I think he was just trying to make me feel good. Lombardi was known as a maniac. He would hit players. My coaching style was more humane.

My athletic scholarship was for football. I played all four years. After my sophomore year, we had nothing but losing seasons. At that point we no longer had players like Charlie Justice or Art Weiner.

My scholarship provided for room, board, books, tuition, and fifteen dollars a month for laundry. I very seldom used the fifteen dollars for laundry. I washed my clothes in the shower. I was also getting twenty-five dollars a month from Dr. McCoy and Dr. Stokes, UNC alumni. They'd helped recruit me and offered a little extra inducement to play for the school. I didn't have a penny to my name, and at that time it was common practice to offer a player incentives. Now it's completely illegal. Coach Snavely did find out about it and had the doctors' money sent to the athletic department.

When I went to Chapel Hill, I had peg pants and a couple of sweaters. All of the veterans wore Army-Navy clothes to class. I saw that as the dress code. Guys wore pea coats, khaki pants, army jackets, and boondockers (a high military boot). When I saw that, I immediately went out to the Army-Navy store and used money from my laundry allowance to buy khaki pants, a pea coat, and boondockers. I wanted to look like everyone else on campus.

My freshman year was easier for me academically than for many other students. My high school education in Portsmouth had prepared me for college. I'd had college algebra and trigonometry and was writing papers with footnotes. Many students from North Carolina hadn't had the high caliber of teachers that I had. North Carolina has more small towns than any other state in the country and the small-town schools were not great. Admission to the university was guaranteed if you graduated from high school in North Carolina. Many who arrived there were not prepared for college.

The only thing that I was really worried about was math. To make sure I was ready, I hired a tutor to help me to be prepared during that summer before college. I was working as a flagman at Military Highway Overpass. I made 75 cents an hour and worked ten hours a day. I paid Miss Culpepper, my high school math teacher, $1.25 an hour to tutor me in college Algebra. I worked with her for a few hours two nights a week for the entire summer in order to prepare for Chapel Hill.

My drive to succeed in college never faltered. Saying to myself, *I may not be as smart as some of these people, but I can outwork anyone here.* I was up at five every morning studying for two hours before my eight o'clock class.

During my first year, I lived with three guys in one room with two double bunks. They were all veterans of WWII. Coach Snavely wanted his players to stay with other students rather than in an athletic dorm. He wanted them to become a part of campus life. That first year, when I came in at night I didn't open my mouth to anyone who was studying. Sometimes we'd have a record player going to study for a class in classical music appreciation.

My sophomore year I roomed with two football players. That dorm was so noisy that I spent my hours at night studying in the library.

I had a roommate named Glenn Nickerson from Boston. His nickname was Black Nick because he had really black hair. He played end in college. He was my best friend and roommate in college. We went in the marines together, and he was the best man at my wedding. Some guys came in on football scholarships from Philadelphia and said that I looked like a baseball player named Spider Jorgenson, who played for the Philadelphia Athletics, so they called me Spider. After that, nobody on campus knew my first name. I was known as Spider for the last three years of college. I started thinking, *I'll be so glad to get off of this campus and get to a place where people know my name.* In the class of '52 directory they had a picture of me and underneath it said, *William O'Brien. Known as Spider.*

My roommate my sophomore year at Carolina was Leon (Bud) Carson, who later became the defensive coordinator for the Pittsburgh Steelers. They won four straight Super Bowls. He planned to major in business, but

I changed his mind. I told him what one of my history professors said. The professor told the class if you're going to do something forty hours a week, you better enjoy it because all of a sudden thirty years are up and you haven't enjoyed your life. I said to him, "If you're going to do something, Bud, you better enjoy it." I knew that he loved coaching. I talked him into becoming a coach and he'll admit it. Bud's defense was one of the best in the NFL.

One of my best professors was Kermit Hunter. He taught me English composition. He wrote a pageant called "Horn in the West" that is performed every year in Boone, North Carolina. He wanted me to go to Boone and become an Indian in the pageant. I turned him down because I had a job running a summer camp up in Kent County. I got room, board, and three hundred dollars cash for eight weeks of work. Years later I wondered if I might have become an actor instead of a coach had I taken his offer.

At the very end of my four years I needed one three-hour class to graduate so I stayed for a three-week summer class. I took a class on North Carolina history. It was the worst class I ever took. I went to the professor and said, "I need three hours to graduate. I just want a C, not a see-me." He laughed. I ended up getting a B.

I had been in the Marine Corps reserve in high school for two years. When I went to UNC the first thing the coaches did was have every player join either the Naval Reserve Officers Corps (Navy ROTC) or the Air Force ROTC. In 1950, when the Korean War started, the entire Marine Corps Reserve that Coach Esleeck had had us join went to war. Only the players who went to college didn't go.

One recruiter knew all of the football players and got half of the football players in my class to go to the Officer Candidate Course at Quantico, Virginia. When I graduated from college I went into the marines.

MY YEARS IN THE MARINE CORPS

In the summer of 1952, after three weeks of summer school at the University of North Carolina, I had finally attained my degree. I packed my bags and got a ride from a fellow student who had an old Packard. He was headed for St. Louis and I was going to Conway, Missouri, where my parents were living in retirement. The Packard broke down twice on the road to St. Louis, but we made it. I hitchhiked from St. Louis to Conway. Back in those days we hitchhiked everywhere.

I stayed a few weeks with my parents and then I had to report to Quantico, Virginia. I was glad to see my parents but didn't like that part of Missouri. It was in the Ozarks. It was hills and unpaved roads and nothing to do. Everybody had pick-up trucks with their names painted on the side of the door. I didn't even have a driver's license but I drove around. There was no place to go but to the country store, and even that was not any fun because I felt like a city boy. When the time came to go, I presented the orders to report to Quantico at the train station and got a free train ticket.

Quantico is in Virginia, about fifteen miles from Washington, D.C. The Officer Candidate Course was at Brown Air Field. We stayed in barracks and got up at 5:30 a.m. and did not go to bed at night until 11:30. They made sure we were doing something all the time. We had been at OCC for about six weeks, and one Saturday morning after marching, passing in review, and singing the Marine Corps Hymn, Sgt. Harry Sinclair, our drill instructor began yelling at us. He said, "I want all of you jar heads to go into Washington, D.C., and I want you to get drunk and have a good time. I don't want to see you messing around with any Doggies [Army] or Swabbies [Navy]."

At that time a member of the 3rd platoon raised his hand and said, "Sgt. Sinclair, my brother is coming to meet me in Washington and he is in the navy."

Sergeant Sinclair shouted, " Dammit boy, he had better look like you." I don't think he had any intention of following us to Washington. The young marine that asked the question failed out of OCC about two weeks later.

After graduating from Officer Candidate Course, I became a second lieutenant in the USMCR. We then began six months of basic training.

We learned to drill and fired weapons. We learned to fire every weapon in the Marine Corps—M1s, carbines howitzers, 60 mm and 81 mm mortars, as well as flame-throwers. It was mostly about seeing if we would obey orders and seeing if we could take the pressure. I'd been hollered at all of my life by coaches, so the yelling didn't even bother me. A marine will always remember his or her drill instructor. Mine was Harry Sinclair.

After graduation from Basic School, I was sent to Camp LeJeune to be in the Amtrack Battalion. Shortly thereafter I was assigned to a reinforced marine battalion, which had howitzers and tanks. We went across the Atlantic to the Mediterranean. We were on the so-called "Med Cruise."

We crossed the Atlantic in January. The waves were so huge they looked three stories high. I was seasick for a solid week. It took about two weeks to cross the ocean. Our first port of entry was in Oran, Algiers. At that time they were controlled by the French. The main fort of the French Foreign Legion was located in Sidi Bell Adbes. We went to Oran to get fresh water, fruits, and vegetables. Docked next to us was a French luxury liner. The entire French Foreign Legion was marched onto this ship.

They wore white hats, blue coats, and black boots with the pants tucked into their boots. A band played the Marseilles over and over as the Legionnaires marched onto the vessel. It was a most emotional and moving experience for me.

I noticed that they had bolt-action 03 Springfield rifles. Those were obsolete even in WWII. We had M1s and semiautomatic carbines that could be set on automatic.

When I asked someone where the Legionnaires were going, they told me that they were going to Vietnam to help the French at Dien Ben Piu. About 90 percent of the French Foreign Legion that I watched board that ship were either captured or killed by the Viet Cong.

We made landings on Sardinia, Turkey, and Greece in preparation for working with the NATO forces. Around April the entire marine battalion was placed on alert. We were given ammunition for our rifles and .45s. We started to sail for Indochina to bail the French out of Dien Ben Piu. After sailing for about a week and a half, we were taken off of alert.

I later found out that the French had been begging us to help them. President Eisenhower sent Secretary of State John Foster Dulles to talk to British Prime Minister Winston Churchill, asking the British to help us assist the French. Prime Minister Churchill replied that in no way were the British going to help the French out of a situation that they had caused. "If the British won't help," our president said, "we will not enter." That is when our ship turned around and sailed back to the States.

We returned to Camp LeJeune, North Carolina. I talked to Benny Walser, a former UNC teammate and friend, who was coaching the football team at Camp LeJeune. He asked my colonel if I could play football for the team. The colonel agreed.

Even though we were at war, every base had a football team to help boost morale. Camp LeJeune is near Jacksonville. The camp is a million miles wide and the only thing they had in Jacksonville at that tine were beer joints. I'm saying this in jest, but, that's how it appeared to me.

I made first-team offensive left end and we won our first two games. In the third game, against the Little Creek Amphibious Base team, the Gators, I caught a hook pass and turned to run. Their right defensive back tackled me by driving his helmet into my left thigh. The hit caused a hematoma. The muscle in my thigh ruptured and my leg swelled to twice the size of my right leg. They pumped coagulated blood out of my thigh for weeks.

After the injury, I was assigned back to the Amtrack Battalion. I reported to Colonel Thomas Johnson. He asked me to coach the battalion football team. I was on crutches; however, I eagerly said that I would do it. The injury didn't seem too pleasant, but in recollection, it was a fortunate thing as I got to coach football.

I showed up on a hot afternoon on crutches wearing a khaki summer uniform. The colonel of the Amtrack Battalion brought me before the team and announced that I was the new coach. I felt so great. This was a moment that I had dreamed of.

The first thing that I did was run a practice and set up offensive plays using the split-T formation which had been made famous by Jim Tatum of the University of Maryland and coach Bud Wilkerson of the University of Oklahoma. I had played for the University of North Carolina, but we were imitating the University of Maryland's offense. I was already applying skills I had acquired in college and moving the team to a higher level of play.

I only had a week to prepare for my first game as a coach. I worked on building a strong running offense. Here I was, the team coach, a guy on crutches, and not much older than many of the guys I was coaching. Most of the guys had duties in the Marine Corps so we only practiced in the afternoon. They were tough but had been poorly coached.

We played on weekdays. There was hardly anybody there to watch the games except a few officers and men from the battalion. We won the first game. I had that split-T going and nobody knew how to stop it.

For the next seven games, we couldn't be stopped. We dominated every game. I felt elated. I was in complete control.

We played a Court House Bay Battalion for the Battalion Championship of Camp LeJeune. Chief Warrant Officer Joe Tusa, an original Wake Island defender, requested that a Marine Corps band play at the game. I guess they couldn't turn down a man who had survived all of WWII in a Japanese Prison Camp. The Colonel had the entire battalion in the stands, and the band played the Marine Hymn. My football team kicked butts and won 27–0.

After that, I was asked to become a regular and keep on coaching the team. I was married and had an infant son. I felt like I wasn't moving ahead toward what I really wanted to do: coaching and teaching in high school. I turned down the offer and left the Marine Corps.

Getting the Great Bridge High School Coaching Job

Returning to Portsmouth, Virginia, in November 1954, after two years in the Marine Corps, I applied for a job at Norfolk County Schools, which later became the Chesapeake School System.

Even though the school year had already started, I was very lucky because there was an open position teaching government and history at Great Bridge High School. I had minored in history at Chapel Hill, so I was qualified. I was able to start teaching within a week.

Great Bridge High School was a new school, just opening that school year. It was in a rural area to the south of Portsmouth, about fifteen miles from the North Carolina border. There were about fifteen hundred students. It's very different now than it was in those days. The area around the school is now heavily developed. There are million-dollar homes all over the place. One of the reasons people began moving to the area was because of the great school system. When I started teaching and coaching, I could look from the school into cornfields because the school had been built on a farm.

When I was at Chapel Hill, I had been told by a college professor that you should pick out the toughest student in the school and nail him to the cross in order to establish your authority. When I started teaching, I intended to demand discipline such as I was accustomed to in the Marine Corps.

The first guy to challenge was a freshman student named Lincoln Pratt. He was short and mean looking. He had dark hair in a crew cut. He was the only student who hadn't turned in his report card.

I said, "Bring in your report card signed by your parents tomorrow." He replied, "I will if I can remember." I repeated more forcefully what I had already said. Again he said, "I will if I can remember." I grabbed him by the shoulder, "Come with me to the principal's office."

I already knew the principal, Douglas Eley, but I didn't know him really well. He backed me up completely. He said, "Lincoln Pratt, get your books out of your locker. You're suspended for two days. And bring your parents with you when you come back."

I had been at the school for only half an hour and I had already suspended one of the toughest kids in the school. It quickly spread through the student body that you better not mess with O'Brien. Linky became one of my best players on the football team and was awarded a scholarship to the University of Richmond. We're still friends to this day.

Toward the end of the school year, I helped Bob Zoll, the coach of the track team, as an assistant coach. We defeated Churchland High School. It was the first time that Great Bridge had defeated Churchland in anything in ten years. The principal of the school noticed that we had won in the shot put, high jump, and discus throw. These were the events that I took part in as captain of the Wilson track team.

I had established myself as a good coach. I found out at the end of the school year that all three coaching positions at Great Bridge were open—track, football, and basketball. I wanted those coaching jobs. I had applied at two other schools for a coaching job but had not heard from either.

I applied formally to Doug Eley, but he said that I was too young (twenty-five years old). They had offered the jobs to three or four people; however, nobody had accepted then. The school was out in the boondocks. There was no housing, only a pool hall, a grocery store, and a confectionery.

My wife, Joyce, and I had become good friends with the principal, Doug Eley, and his wife, Evelyn. There was time for a short vacation before I started worrying about how I was going to make some money over the summer. The Eleys had planned a vacation week at Nag's Head, North Carolina, and asked if we would like to share the cottage with them.

Doug loved to talk about sports. Many hours were spent that week talking about our experiences at Woodrow Wilson High School. He had played basketball at the University of Richmond and had coached basketball at Great Bridge when he first came there as a teacher.

It was a great week, but I was hoping for an answer about the coaching jobs. The last night we were there, we all had a few stiff drinks and I asked about the position. Doug was in a very mellow mood and said, "All right. You're head coach of football, basketball, and track. And you had better win."

Head Coach — My First Year

After successfully obtaining the Great Bridge High School football coaching job, I was so excited. All those boyhood dreams had come true. Thinking of all the possible ways to be successful in my chosen career consumed most of my every thought. I was twenty-five years old and a head coach. How I wanted to have a winning season.

During the summer of 1955, I took five of the best Great Bridge players to Camp Kentwood as counselors but also wanted to have a chance to work with them on football skills. Camp Kentwood was a boys camp for kids, ages from six–fourteen. It was located in Kent County, Virginia, about twenty miles from Richmond. There's a horse racing track near there now and the camp is a park.

I had previously gone to Camp Kentwood while in high school and college. The camp was owned by my good friend, Rhae Adams' aunt. Rhae got me a job as junior counselor. After the first year, I became a senior counselor and my senior year in high school, I became waterfront director. During my freshman year at UNC, Mrs. Woodson appointed me camp director.

I worked with the players on football in the evenings. I also coached some of the campers that were interested in football. We threw passes and played touch football. All of these players were on the first team that fall. This summer training was the beginning of what eventually became my famous marine camp summer training, which started in 1960.

One of the players in that first camp, Bob Lemmon, got a football scholarship at University of Richmond. One of the things that I taught him that summer was how to be a T-quarterback. He had been a tailback the previous year in a single wing.

For a week before classes started in the fall of 1955, I instituted two-a-day practices, something that no one had ever done before at Great Bridge. I ended up kicking half of the players off of the team, including Lincoln Pratt, who became one of the greatest athletes I ever coached. If you didn't show up for practice, you were off for the rest of the season.

Our practices were at eight in the morning and four in the afternoon. Once classes started we just practiced in the afternoon.

We started practicing on about August 25, and our first game was the second week in September. I had about twenty-five players. We played

Coach Billy O'Brien. Photo by Lonney Johnson, *Virginian Pilot*.

Edenton in North Carolina.

It was a memorable game. We were beaten 35–0; it was awful. I just about got in a fight with someone after the game because I'd kicked Lincoln Pratt off of the team for missing practice.

The previous season Churchland had beaten Great Bridge 60–0 in football. After I took over as coach I made a statement to the press that we would never be beaten like that again. That statement came back to haunt me. We played Churchland in the middle of the season. They had a running back named John Saunders. Charles "Shotgun" Brown, the coach of their team, never took Saunders out of the game for the entire four quarters. He scored six touchdowns. We were trounced 60–0. I'm not sure if we even made a first down the entire game. I was completely devastated. I remember going home and not being able to sleep the entire night after that game. The next day I fainted in the living room of our apartment.

I remember looking at the game film and saw some of my first-team players hiding under the bench, not wanting to go back into the game. I truly believe that episode was the worst experience I've ever had in any football career.

I recall that in the practice after that game, I'd donned a helmet and shoulder pads with the intent of teaching my players how to tackle. If a coach would do something like that today, he'd probably be fired. I tackled one young man in the practice and hit him so hard that he quit the team.

We struggled on and were able to win three games out of the ten. I recall beating Deep Creek 41–0 and thinking I saw something that might be good in the future.

After football I went immediately into coaching basketball and had a losing season. At that time we were Group 2, and the away games took us to Franklin and Smithfield. We had a girls' team, a JV team, and a varsity team. We'd leave on a school bus and go fifty or sixty miles away and play three basketball games. We were getting home at one or two in the morning. Eight o'clock classes seemed awfully early the next day.

After that year I never coached basketball again. I enjoyed as much of that as I could stand.

Track season rolled around and I had everyone who was going to participate in football on the track team. We had my unwritten rule at Great Bridge. If you wanted to be on the football team, you had better be on the track team. You could go out for baseball your senior year.

I taught all of the players how to sprint and taught the tackles and guards how to throw the discus and shot put. I had all the ends learning the high jump. The sprinters were taught how to broad jump. I didn't put much emphasis on distance running like the mile and half mile. I wanted sprinters on my team and shot putters in the line. The most amazing thing of that year is that we beat Churchland in track and they were coached by Shotgun Brown.

GREAT BRIDGE HIGH SCHOOL'S
FIRST WRESTLING TEAMS

After going through a losing season in basketball, I resigned from that position with the concept in my mind that I would start a wrestling team the next year. While at UNC, I had taken a course in wrestling in physical education and had wrestled in the intramural program. I felt that I did have some knowledge of the sport.

It was not my intention to have a great wrestling team but instead to have all my football players who did not play basketball to participate in the wrestling program.

At that time, there were three schools that had wrestling teams; they were Granby, Maury, and Norview. Having no equipment, I borrowed a wrestling mat from Bo Lo Perdue, Norview's principal. We practiced in football jerseys and pants. Doug Eley, our principal, bought us a set of game wrestling uniforms. I had thirty football players on my first wrestling team. Matches were scheduled with the JV teams playing each team twice. All matches were scheduled during the fifth and sixth period of the day. Some of the teachers were unhappy about the students missing their classes, but in those days the principal of the school ruled the roost.

We charged each student ten cents to come to the match, and those who did not have a dime were let in free. They went crazy over the team as they had never seen a wrestling match before. Thus, wrestling was born at Great Bridge.

The day after our first match, a student came up to me and said, "Coach, you better go over to the girls' gym and see what's going on." I proceeded to do just that. The PE teachers had the girls wrestling. In absolute amazement, I told them that this would have to stop immediately. As chairman of the Physical Education Department, I did have authority to do this. It was not difficult to imagine the reaction of the girls' parents when they heard of this.

We discontinued the "during school" meets and soon began scheduling meets with other schools as they too began a wrestling program.

In 1960 Johnny Thompson finished second in the state meet against Ken Whitley's Norview team. Johnny graduated from the University of

Florida on a football scholarship. He is now a very famous author and has written many books.

Needing to improve my track team, I turned the wrestling over to Sandy Jarrel. Sandy was an English teacher at Great Bridge. He had previously taught at Granby and worked with the famous wrestling coach Billy Martin. Not only did he do a good job with the wrestling, he became one of the best JV line coaches I ever had.

I want to say thanks to Billy Martin, who taught me and my team the Granby Roll and many other holds.

Great Bridge High School, since those early days, has become one of the best wrestling teams in the USA due to the sons of Billy Martin who have coached the teams.

SECOND YEAR COACHING —
MY FIRST WINNING SEASON

As we started the next season in 1956, I was sure that I was a good coach, but I knew that it didn't look that way.

I no longer had to kick anyone off the team because they knew what to expect of me. The players knew that they couldn't miss practice and they had to do what I told them to do in the game. They were on my side.

Our opening game was against Edenton in North Carolina. They had won fifty games in a row. We outplayed them the entire game. At the end of the game, we were leading 13–12. I said to myself, *We're going home with a victory.*

They drove the ball down to our four-yard line with six seconds to play and no time outs. The head official was a local jewelry store owner and also the official time keeper in the game. They ran three running plays in six seconds and beat us. The next day I called him long-distance and chewed him out.

Our next game was with Craddock. We ran up twenty-one first downs and scored one touchdown. Craddock was coached by Larry Weldon, a former Washington Redskins quarterback who knew a lot about the passing game. We were beaten 35–7 by their passing game.

We'd lost two in a row. I said to myself, *Here it goes again.*

The next week we played Virginia Beach, which was coached by Fred Isaaks. He was probably second only to Shotgun Brown in winning seasons in the whole Tidewater District.

The Wednesday night before the game, I went to a Marine Reserve meeting. Jack Mounie, a friend from my high school years and former captain of the Duke University football team, was also there. I told him that our defense stunk. He diagrammed a defense and suggested that we try it. It was a split-6 defense that had been used against Chapel Hill while I was there.

At Thursday practice we put in the new defense. We took all of the backs and ends who were fast and tough and put six in the line and two were linebackers. The rest were three deep. I put all of my fat, slow guards and tackles on the bench. We stopped Virginia Beach cold in that game. They only beat us on an intercepted pass in the final quarter. It was 7–0 at the end.

23

I had now completed thirteen games in my tenure as a Great Bridge football coach. The upcoming game was with Churchland, who had beaten us 60–0 in my first year as coach.

I told my wife that if we didn't win the Churchland game, I was going to get another job. I'd already applied at several pharmaceutical companies and farm equipment companies to become a salesman. It had to be better than coaching football and certainly would pay more money.

We played Churchland on a homecoming Friday night with a large, boisterous crowd of our school's fans. We hadn't beaten Churchland in fifteen years. The fans didn't think we had a chance, and probably half of them were just coming to look at the floats in the parade at halftime and to see who would be the homecoming queen. Most students had a pretty good idea about the queen because only the football team voted for the homecoming queen. In my twenty years as coach, the homecoming queen was always a girlfriend of one of the stars on the football team.

Our team was very determined. We had a new defense that had worked well in the last game, but Churchland was undefeated after three games in the season. They had a great running game, and I knew we had to stop that part of their game.

I was delighted to see our defense working perfectly and stopping their running game, but our offense was terrible. The first half was a punting game with no score. The second half was about the same except that Lincoln Pratt went thirty-six yards off tackle and scored, knocking at least four Churchland players on the ground. Our second score was a forty-five-yard touchdown pass caught by Johnny Cooke. Our defense worked perfectly. They never got past our forty-yard line the entire game.

We won the game 14–0 and the fans went berserk and rushed out on the field. The players carried me around the field on their shoulders. Had there been a mayor and such a position in Great Bridge, I could've been elected mayor the following day.

We had a party that night at our principal's house that lasted until three o'clock in the morning with the coaches, wives, and friends like Dick Davis, our announcer, and T.T. Turner, an English teacher who was in charge of editing the yearbook.

This was a turning point for the team and for my life. We won the next six games and finished with a seven-win three-losses season. Churchland only beat us once in the next eighteen years. Shotgun Brown quit coaching after that season and became a salesman for a sporting goods company.

I never thought about becoming a salesman again. I had fulfilled a dream that went back to when I was eight years old and playing in the community leagues in Portsmouth. I knew that I had the ability to coach winning teams and achieve victory. Even when I was in the state legislature, they called me Coach. I was proud of that and my winning record.

THE BACK-TO-BACK RAIN GAMES

Part of coaching is making sure that your team gets to play on a level playing field—and a dry one. Our team was small and fast, and a soaking wet field was the worst place for us to play. Opposing teams prayed for rain.

The first time we lost in the rain was in 1960. We had won eight games and were undefeated. We went into the game with Maury on Foreman Field in Norfolk. It rained so hard that you couldn't see the players across the field, even with lights on. We lost 12–0. After that every team wanted to play us in the rain. This lasted throughout my coaching career.

In 1961 it had been raining all week when I got a call on a Thursday. We were scheduled to play Oscar Smith the next day. Bob Zoll, a former track coach at Great Bridge and a friend from my high school days, called me at six-thirty that morning, "Billy, they're watering down the field at Oscar Smith High School."

I jumped into my station wagon and drove over to pick up Jimmy Calhoun, my assistant coach. We arrived at the Oscar Smith field at 7:00 a.m., just as it was starting to get light. The gates to the field were locked so we climbed over a hurricane fence to get onto the field. Water was standing on the grass. If we stepped down hard, mud splashed everywhere. The school band was practicing away from the field because it was too wet for them to use. I told the band director to get the principal of the school so I could talk to him about the condition of the field.

In a few minutes, the principal, Ed Drew, and the superintendent of schools, Ed Brickel, walked up to me. Brickel was the meanest superintendent of schools in the history of South Norfolk, which only had one high school, Oscar Smith. Ed had been a teacher and baseball coach who had gone to the University of Chicago. Ed was highly intelligent, an outstanding educator, and very personable. He was about six feet tall. I stand six-foot-three. He yelled at me, "You son of bitch. What the hell are you doing on my field?"

I said, "That's a fine way to talk to someone in front of these band students."

He said, "Bring your team out. We'll kick your ass."

We started bumping up against each other and I was about to hit him. As a former marine captain, I didn't take a lot of shit from anybody.

25

I said, "We're not coming to play." I turned to my assistant coach and said, "Let's go, Jimmy. We're out of here."

We climbed back over the fence, got in my car, and drove directly to Great Bridge High School. Harry Paxton, Doug Eley, and Ed Brickel were sitting in Eley's office.

Brickel said, "I can get that field in shape so we can play the game. "

I told them we'd be there, but I was still furious.

My friend, Doug pulled open a desk drawer, took out a small bottle, gave me a pill, and said, "This is a Valium. Go home and take one and be back for practice by this afternoon."

Friday night the field was still soaking wet. Our fast offense was bogged down on the muddy field. We ended up in a tie, 13–13 against a team that we should've beaten by a big margin.

On Monday after that weekend, Doug called me into his office and said, "Billy, you are a teacher, a coach, and you climb over fences. You almost got in a fight with the superintendent. You just can't do that."

I said, "You're right. I won't do it again."

The next week we played Warwick. It was pouring rain and lightning was flashing in the sky everywhere. We were out trying to have a pre-game warm-up.

Doug came out on the field and said, "You're not playing under these conditions, are you?"

I said, "You'll have to go up to the press box and talk to their principal because he told me that if we didn't play the game, it will be a forfeit and they will win the game." The rules stated that the home team could decide whether to play.

He walked off in the rain, climbed over a low cyclone fence, and tore a big rip in his raincoat. Then he climbed up into the stands and into the press box. When I looked up at the press box, I could see Doug and the home team principal were shoving each other and shouting.

We started playing the game. By ten minutes into the game, they'd scored a touchdown and blocked a punt for a safety.

I looked up into the sky and thought, *This just isn't fair*. A second later a bolt of lightning hit one of those big banks of field lights above the press box and sparks flew everywhere, just like in *The Natural* when Robert Redford hit a home run into the lights.

The field went black. It was raining hard. I couldn't see the players, stadium seats, the crowd, or even my hand in front of my face. Somehow Doug found me on that field and said, "Get the players on the bus and go back to Great Bridge and we'll come back on Monday night and kick their butts."

We lost eighteen rain hoods that night. We made it to the bus and drove home on dark streets in the pouring rain. On Monday we went back and beat them 38–0 in a new game. On Tuesday morning, I went right to

Doug's office. I looked at him and said, "Doug, you're principal of the high school, a leader in the community. You're climbing over fences. You almost got into a fight with a principal of a school. You just can't be doing that."

He said, "You got me." He was smiling when he added, "Okay, now get the hell out of my office."

Racism

In 1967 I experienced the greatest prevalence of racism that existed in the Eastern District in that day and time. I was born in Parsons, Kansas, and the first black person that I ever saw was when I came to Portsmouth, Virginia, in 1936.

In 1953 the Supreme Court of our country ruled that black children could integrate into the segregated school system that prevailed at that time. A young black man by the name of Washington Johnson was a student at I.C. Norcom High School, a black high school, who transferred to Craddock High School and became a member of the football team.

We played our first game against Princess Anne High School, and we tied the game six to six. I've heard that a tie is like kissing your sister, but it is better than a kick in the butt. The next week we played Craddock and defeated them 38 to 10. We finished with a record of 9 wins, 0 losses, and 1 tie that season.

The season was almost over when Craddock played Granby and defeated them. This defeat left the Granby team with a record of 9 wins and 1 loss. The District Championship was to have been awarded to my Great Bridge team.

How wrong I was. The principals of the Eastern District called a meeting of the coaches and principals at Craddock High School. The topic of the evening was the eligibility of Washington Johnson, the young black man. The Virginia High School League had a transfer rule which states that if a student transfers from one high school to another without a change of address, he must complete one semester of school prior to be eligible to participate in any athletic team.

At the meeting, a principal's opening statement was, "The federal government has said that we must allow the black students to attend our schools, but I don't think we should encourage them to participate in athletics."

They then turned the attention of the meeting to the eligibility of Washington Johnson, who had played defensive end for Craddock. The principals ruled Johnson ineligible for the season. Granby was made the winner of the Craddock game, and its win and loss record went to 10 and 0. Just that easily, a District Championship for Great Bridge vanished.

A lawyer approached me and said that that decision was illegal and would be overturned if taken to court. He offered to pursue this matter free for me without legal fees. I went to Doug Eley, my principal, with this information, and we got into a very heated argument over this ruling. He indicated to me that he was the principal and I was the coach and that he ran the school. Granby won the District Football Championship. About two months later the Department of Health and Welfare reversed the transfer rule of the VHSL and declared that these students were eligible upon matriculating to the school.

At a capricious moment, I think that maybe one day I'll hire a lawyer, take that case to court, and bring that trophy out of Granby High School to the halls of Great Bridge High School where it rightly belongs.

The Virginian-Pilot
Friday, November 19, 1965
Abe Goldblatt's
Prep Picks

THE WASHINGTON JOHNSON CASE: I am well aware of the fact that the Virginia High School League had no alternative but to declare Cradock's Washington Johnson ineligible. A rule is a rule, but in Johnson's case—and all others like it—I think it is unique.

Much has happened in our way of living since the rule was written into the VHSL books about two decades ago. The most revolutionary development in our system has been the integration of public schools.

The rule has never been revised to cover the problems brought about the integration.

Last spring every public school pupil in Portsmouth was given the choice of school he wished to attend in September. Because Cradock was closer to his home than Norcom, an all-Negro high school, Johnson selected Cradock.

The VHSL transfer rule states: "He shall not have enrolled in one high school and subsequently transferred to and enrolled in another high school without a corresponding change in the residence of his parents, parent, or guardian."

In such a case, a transfer student becomes eligible for interschool competition after he has completed one full semester of attendance at the high school to which he has transferred.

In Johnson's case, however, he was given his freedom of choice like all other students in the city. Then why should he and his school be penalized? I imagine he would be permitted to play in the Craddock band or take part in other school activities. But varsity athletics are forbidden to him until next year.

Washington, no doubt, is mystified by it all. So is his principal, J.J. Booker, Jr., who has always been a stickler for the enforcing of all VHSL laws. Like a lot of other folks, I am sure Mr. Booker felt the transfer rule didn't cover a student who moved to another school under jurisdiction approved by the school board.

The VHSL must amend some of its ancient laws governing athletics to meet the changing times.

Craddock has had to forfeit all its wins this season because Johnson was declared ineligible. Some good may come of it, though. Granby, as a result, now finds itself unbeaten. If the Comets beat Maury on Thanksgiving Day they'll play Annandale for the State title. We've always said that best football in the State is played in the Eastern District. Now's the time to prove it.

CURTIS HALL, JOEY O'BRIEN, AND HAIR

When I arrived in my new job as head coach for football, basketball, and track, most all of the players had crew cuts, including me, as that was the standard for the U.S. Marine Corps from whence I came.

Before I comment further on haircuts, we should go back to examine what occurred to cause me to go through the worst nightmare of my coaching career at Great Bridge High School.

When the Beatles came to America with their music and long hair, every young man in the United States stopped liking crew cuts. I know the young ladies did not want to date short-haired young men.

Our school board had issued an edict that long-haired young men could not be tolerated in our schools. Then some parent took that edict to the Supreme Court and that was overruled.

What happened was every boy at every school in our system wanted to have long hair, but being from the old school, all of our coaches, including myself said, "If you are going to be on any Great Bridge team, you will have short hair—period."

Then the walls came down!

My son, Joey, good athlete, good student, loved me and his mother, started to grow his hair long. I told him in no uncertain terms to go to the barber shop. He did as I requested and later when he came home with his haircut, I did not approve of the length. "You go back to the shop and get some more hair cut off." He was fifteen years old and he started crying like a four-year-old.

I thought to myself, *What in the hell have I done to the most prized possession that I have?* I thought.

That did it! From then on as athletic director of Great Bridge High, if any player on any team behaved in class, did his academic requirements, and performed well in athletics, he could have his hair as long as he desired. Principal Harry Blevins, Assistant James Calhoun, and the JV football coach went ballistic. We went around and around for weeks, but I prevailed. About a year went by and Harry and Jimmy had hair as long as the students. The

Coach Billy O'Brien. Photo by Lonney Johnson, *Virginian Pilot*.

JV football coach, Martin Oliver, was bald.

Curtis Hall played linebacker and offensive right halfback. He was an A student. His father, Herman Hall, was chairman of the school board. His grandfather, Colin Hall, was chairman of the board of supervisors for Norfolk County. The family, being farmers, owned about half of the land in the area.

Curtis was one tough, mean cookie. Before I changed my attitude on hair, I tried to talk him into getting his hair cut. This is a coaching tip that I used on Curtis, but I would not recommend it for all players.

"I have got to find a way to coach this young, talented man." He did not like to take orders from anyone.

Here was my solution. I would suggest things to him. "Curtis, don't you think it might be nice to roll block the stand-up dummy to emulate the block you have to execute on the opposition?" Curtis would reply, "That's a good idea, Coach." We had talks and I made suggestions.

We won the district championship. Curtis made twenty-six tackles on Mike Voight and we defeated Indian River 18–0. Curtis also ran for a thirty-eight-yard touchdown. We held Mike Voight, the leading rusher in the state, to seventeen yards that night. Mike went to the University of North Carolina and holds the record as the third leading ground gainer in the history of UNC football.

Curtis Hall's beautiful brown curly hair was hanging six inches out of the back of his helmet the entire evening.

THE GREAT BRIDGE FOOTBALL PLAYER LIST

I received a call from Bill Leffler, a retired sportswriter, and he requested that I send him a list of the best players that I coached thirty years ago.

I thought, *How in the hell could I be fair to all those I had coached?* I began searching my mind for an answer. I sent Bill list of thirty-three names. He chose four and printed their names: Ken Barefoot, best pro I coached, David Unser, captain of Duke football team as best college player; Linky Pratt, best football player; and Fella Rhodes as best athlete.

When I saw the article I almost started crying as I thought I had hurt the feelings of a lot of players I truly loved.

I will start with Ronney Lowery, defensive and offensive end. He was a full-blooded Lumbee Indian. Some believe the Lumbee intermarried with the members of the Lost Colony because many of them had English last names.

Once, we were playing Woodrow Wilson of Portsmouth, Virginia. During the second half of the game, one of the officials came to our bench and told me to come out on the field. I went with him to the middle of the field. Ron Lowery had a compound fracture of his left forearm. The bone was protruding out of the skin. He had made about seven plays on defense and refused to leave the game. "You come with us to the bench and I'm sending you to the hospital."

Before he graduated, I took him to Chapel Hill with some game films of his play, and when I told the UNC coach about that incident, he brought out the papers and signed Ronnie to a four-year football scholarship.

Ronnie played first-team defensive halfback for UNC and graduated. He runs an oil rig in Louisiana.

Tommy Rhodes was the best quarterback I ever coached and would have made the pros but went to the wrong school. I took him and his parents to Georgia Tech where my friend Bud Carson was head coach. They were using a drop back passing offense and wanted to sign him while we were there.

He changed his mind and went to the University of South Carolina. They used a sprint out offense that needed a running quarterback. He later became a great high school coach and is now an elementary principal.

One family in Great Bridge contributed so much to the success of the football program, it would be impossible to ever give the credit that they so richly deserve. The Unser family gave me David and Richard to coach. These two young men were good students. They behaved in class, they ran track, and they were perfect gentlemen.

David was a fullback during my first winning season. I moved him to guard on defense where he was largely responsible for the defense. Those seasons kept me in the coaching profession.

David had not received much attention from the press and no colleges were recruiting him. I made up my mind that I was going to get him into UNC with a football scholarship. I borrowed a game film from Shot Gun Brown and off we went to Chapel Hill.

I gave Jim Tatum, UNC's head coach, the most persuasive speech that I had ever made, and he wanted to sign him that moment. David felt he needed to talk to his parents before signing. So home we went.

Ace Parker, the greatest athlete ever to come from Virginia, was an assistant coach at Duke. When he found out that I wanted David to go to UNC, he went after David. David entered Duke University on a four-year scholarship and played first-team end on defense and offense for three years. He was elected captain of the Duke football team his senior year. That year Duke received an invitation to the Cotton Bowl and played against Arkansas. David blocked an extra-point attempt which allowed Duke to win the Cotton Bowl 7 to 6.

Maxine Unser, the boys' mother, drove the athletic bus and took the players to all of the away games. I don't know what I would have done without her. She was like a mother to the entire team.

Lawrence Unser, their father, learned to operate our film camera and took all our game films for fifteen years. After the game, he would drive to Norfolk where the film was to be dropped off. The developing would be completed by Saturday morning for pick up so I could have it for review on Saturday and Sunday.

Richard Unser was a guard his senior year and we lost our first three games. We changed our wing-T offense to a four-in-the-I offense. We moved Richard to blocking back and we won the next seven games. He made All-Tidewater and received a four-year ride to Duke.

They were some family

This is the original list as I submitted to Bill Leffler.

* Best Football Player: Linky Pratt, University of Richmond
* Best Athlete: Fella Rhodes, East Carolina University
* Best College Player: David Unser, captain, Duke University

* Best Pro-Football Player: Ken Barefoot, Virginia Tech
* Meanest Football Player: Fred Childress and Allen (Alley Cat) Spencer
* Toughest Football Player: Ron Lowry, University of North Carolina
* Best Pass Receiver: Ron Dunbar, University of Cincinnati
* Best Linebacker: Curtis Hall
* All-Around Football Player: Lora Hinton, LSU
* Best Hands of Any Player I Coached: Stan Eure, East Carolina University
* Best Defensive Back: Richard Johnson
* Best Two Tackles: John Thompson and Red Warren, University of Florida and Elon
* Best Two Guards: Donnie Baker and Steve Sanderlin
* Most Exciting Runner: Joe Bussey, Duke University
* Best Center: Bob Kinnard, East Carolina University
* Best Fullback: Bob Royster, Virginia Tech
* Best Running Back: Allen Hall, East Carolina University
* Best Deep Receiver: Emanuel Upton, Norfolk State
* Most Intelligent Player: Mike Root, MIT
* Most Courageous: Stanley Lancaster, UNC
* Most Deceptive Quarterback: Mickey Ottley
* Best Little Player: Wayne Head—120 pounds
* Most Deceptive Running Back: Raleigh Voight, Virginia Tech
* Fastest Running Back: Jimmy Cutchins, North Carolina State
* Best Running Back That I Almost Missed: Charlie Cristwell
* Best Two High School Coaches I Coached: Lewis Johnson and John Cooke, W&M and VMI
* Best Four-Letterman: Bob Lemmon, University of Richmond
* Only Back Ever to Score Six Touchdowns in One Game: Charlie Olah
* Fastest Player: Frankie Roberson, Tennessee State University (9.6 100 yards)
* Best All-Around End: Jim Tuthill, William and Mary
* Only Lawyer I Coached Who Could Catch a Pass: Steve Comfort, University of Maryland
* Toughest Fullback: David McManus
* Best All-Around Quarterback: Tommy Rhodes, University of South Carolina
* Smallest Best Linebacker: Jimmy Jay Calhoun, Virginia Tech
* Toughest Little End: Jerry Everton, Old Dominion

SOME ADVICE TO COACHES

I'd like to share some techniques that I found particularly helpful during my coaching career.

The first thing that you have to remember is that you're dealing with the child of a parent or parents who feel their child is their most precious possession in the world. Treat that child as you would your own child: with respect, love, and care. Many of my athletes went on to win scholarships to college. I was proud to help make that possible. Education is the number one priority in life. As a coach you are educating them by your example and your words. The other thing to keep in mind is that in ten years, one of those students you coached might end up on the school board.

If you have two players who are about equal in their level of play, here's a way to get the best out of both of them. Send both out of the locker room when all the other players are there. Have paper and pencils ready. Ask the team for a secret vote on who should play by writing down the name of the best player. Take the pieces of paper into your office and toss them into the wastebasket. Bring one of the two players into the locker room and tell him that the team has elected him to play on the team. He's elated because he's been voted to play and will play even better. The other guy wants to prove that his teammates were wrong, so he will play his best game ever.

Alternate these two players so each one plays about fifty percent of the game. You'll get the greatest effort from these two players you've ever seen. As soon as the game is over and you have a victory, take both players into the office and tell the two of them that you never even counted the votes. Congratulate both of them on the great game they've played. You can do this about once every four years.

Coaching is like acting. You have to give a great performance. Don't be afraid to play it up as if you were on stage. Use dramatic techniques to get the most out of your players. If I wanted to bring tears to my eyes and still maintain my composure, I would bring an onion in a baggie to school. Before a game, I would peel it and wrap the onion in a gym towel. When I was talking to the players at half time, I'd pretend to wipe sweat off of my face and actually I'd be holding the onion close to my eyes. The tears would flow. I would tell them how important it was for me to see them win.

Scouting reports can be used to improve the performance of your players, if they're used creatively. Early in my career, I asked the assistant coaches where our players left the scouting reports that we made out each week. They said they just placed them on top of their lockers and never looked at then.

We went to watch a JV game over at a local school where our varsity team was going to play the next week. We found a scouting report their coaches had made about the quality of our players. We found a copy of their scouting report form and took it with us.

Back at our school, we filled in our own written assessments of our players: *Mike Powers—Big, fat, slow tackle. Hit him hard one time and he'll quit the rest of the game. Alleycat Spencer—small, quick guard. Doesn't like to hit. David Unser—fumbles often. When you tackle him try to tear the ball out his hands; it's easy.*

We would show the scouting report to the players. They'd see the report and start teasing the players: "Alley cat doesn't like to hit."

Well, our players were playing like never before. Some went a little too far. Alleycat Spencer went out there and he was trying to kill the other guys. I had to take him out of the game and say, "Alleycat, the other team didn't say that about you. I made it all up. Now go out there and stop trying to kill them."

Protection of the self-image is the greatest motivator of behavior there is. When talking to a player, tell him that you think he's a fine player. Build up his self-image so that when he plays in the game, he will do everything he can to live up to the image you have of him.

I would walk up to players in the hall at school and say, "Are you going to play like I need you to tonight? I think you're the best guard in the whole district." He'll go out there thinking, *I want to prove that the coach is right.*

Fear of consequences is a great deterrent of untoward behavior. Have rules and enforce them, but don't have too many rules.

Teach your players to turn the other cheek. If your opponent hits you with his fist and you retaliate, you will more likely get a fifteen-yard penalty.

Serve officials coffee, Cokes, towels.

Always rate officials high on rating forms.

Never question officials on calls. Think of what play you are going to call with first down and 25.

Never cut a kid—get him a uniform. He might play first-team his senior year.

The next suggestion is the smartest thing I ever did in my coaching career, and it was something we did at UNC the entire four years I was on the team.

Have your pregame warmup and then send twenty-two players to one end of the field for offensive practice and twenty-two players to the other end of the field for defensive practice. As head coach, I was in charge of

Saint Clair Jones, first black coach at Great Bridge High School, and Coach O'Brien.

offense, and I had another coach as head defensive coach.

There are many reasons for this:

1. You never have players standing around with their hands on their hips.
2. All players have a place on the team. They are either first-team offense or first-team defense.
3. At the defense practice you have the second-team defense run the opposing teams offense against the first-team defense, and late in the practice, you allow the first-team defense to run the opposing team's offense. This process is the same for the offensive practice.

   If you have one or two players that you have go both ways, let them spend half of the practice on offense and half on defense. You may have an individual who could start on offense and defense, but if you use him both ways, he will not be as efficient as one who plays just defense and practices for one and a half hours compared to forty-five minutes.
4. Take your team to camp.

The most important player you have on your team is the player who snaps the ball to your punter. That player must practice for thirty minutes of pregame warmup. One year my best punter was also my snapper to the punter. We found another punter. The next most valuable player on your team is the individual who catches the punt from the other team. If you can't find one who you are positive can catch the ball, don't field the punt.

I think punting is something that comes naturally to some people. If you can find that person you are lucky; if you can't find him, take the best football player on your team and teach him to punt. A lot of bad things can happen when you are punting. Also never let a punter take three steps to punt. Two steps are the most he should take.

Before the season, we would have two scrimmages with a high school team that was not on our schedule. If I had two or three key players I knew were good and I was concerned about injury, I would not play them and see how the players who backed them up played.

I was never very successful in teaching how to block punts. We always seemed to rough the kicker.

We never had a full-game scrimmage in practice. Have hard drills for all positions but no full-team scrimmages. Never lose a player in practice to an injury.

In pregame warmup, don't waste time doing calisthenics. Have your team do stretching exercises and then do drills that will be the things they do in a game. You never run automobile tires in a game!

We had a junior high team where seventh and eighth graders played other junior high schools. The seventh- and eighth-grade teams ran my offense and my defense. We had a ninth- and tenth-grade JV team. They ran my offense and defense. These coaches practiced just like we did in every phase of our practice.

When a player came to me as an eleventh grader, he had played in my system for four years. They were easy to coach.

When we were receiving a punt, we would practice setting up a wall for sideline returns. We made sure the wall was five yards from the sideline and players were five yards from each other. When the players were forming the wall, they shouted to each player, "Don't clip, don't clip" all the while they were forming the wall.

We brought about 85 percent of our returns to our sideline. Referees are more reluctant to throw a flag for clipping in front of all of our coaches.

Never do wind sprints after practice, instead have players jog a lap. There are too many chances for pulled muscles in tired legs.

The following procedures are the best secrets that I have ever received from another coach, Julie Conn, of Newport News High School:

How To Teach Your Players To Sprint.
The most important factor in sprinting is relaxation of muscles.

1. Have your sprinter take a very small stone or pebble and place it under his tongue. Have him keep his mouth open when he sprints. This keeps him from tightening up his facial muscles.
2. Have your sprinter place a penny between the thumb and forefingers of each hand. This keeps from locking his fists and keeps his arm muscles relaxed.
3. Make sure he keeps his elbows locked in a 45-degree angle to prevent his arms from folding around his body.
4. Have the runner start out very slow using these procedures. It will seem awkward at first, but do them slowly for about forty yards.

After that have the sprinters do sixty yards in this manner. Run the first twenty yards very slowly and begin to sprint fast the next twenty yards, and for the final twenty yards coast down to slow again. Keep repeating this procedure until it becomes a conditioned reflex and he will not have to think about what he is doing when he sprints very relaxed.

Use Low Hurdles to Teach Sprinters How to Stride.

1. Place four hurdles in the low position. Connect first-aid gauze between the hurdles. When the sprinters' legs hit the gauze, it will not hurt and will not cause the sprinter to fall over the hurdle. Teach them to right leg lead and left leg lead. Have them do the correct drag leg procedure with both the right and left leg. Have the low hurdles set at ten-yard intervals. If the sprinter is short and cannot use the three-stride method as used in high hurdles, let him alternate the right leg lead and left leg lead and do the procedure in four strides. If you have problems with this explanation, consult a track coach and he will explain what I mean.

Teach your sprinters to jump rope like the professional boxers do. This promotes good hand and foot coordination.

THE FOOTBALL GAME PROGRAM

The football program is about the football players, the cheerleaders, the coaches, and the head coach. It is not about the principal, the assistant principals, the band, the superintendent, or the school board.

Grantland Rice said, "When the great scorer comes to mark against your name, it's not whether you won or lost, it's how you played the game." Those are mighty nice words, but that's not the way American sports work.

The way the game is played here is how much money do you make, how many cars did you sell, how many houses did you sell, how many of your students passed the Standards of Learning Exam. The only criteria the people of this country honor is how many games did you win and it better be many more than you lost or you are going to be looking for another job.

My advice to you is to find someone who can write proficiently, and in your football program have him make you, as head coach, the best thing that ever happened to that high school. I have included some of the articles from our football program. It even helped me get elected to the Virginia House of Delegates by twelve thousand votes, even though it was my first time seeking public office. This was the largest margin in the history of the House.

O'BRIEN OBSERVES 15TH ANNIVERSARY, BECOMES No. 1 COACH

If life, as they say, begins at 40, Billy O'Brien is coaching his first football team at Great Bridge this year. Otherwise, this is his 15th season as head coach.

The 40-year-old former University of North Carolina end, who has developed Great Bridge into one of the top football schools in Virginia, didn't realize he had seen 14 teams come and go until he was reminded recently.

"It can't be that many," he said, counting the years on his fingers. "It seems like just yesterday . . ."

Actually, it was in 1954 that O'Brien joined the Great Bridge coaching staff. He was an assistant for one year and has been head coach ever since.

Some of the youthful exuberance may be gone but Billy still retains a remarkable power of concentration for his favorite sport. If you don't believe he is always thinking football, try to talk to him about something else during a practice session.

And if he fails to recognize you when you pass him on the street or in the halls of the school, it's not that he is impolite. He is simply figuring how to get that linebacker to commit himself on the off-tackle play—or how to explain to his wife that he won't be home because of a junior varsity game.

Despite his seeming aloofness, O'Brien hasn't lost many friends during his 15 years at Great Bridge. One of the reasons is that basically he is a friendly, fun-loving person—during the off-season. You should have seen his performance in a Baltimore night spot about three years ago. He had 10 Colt fans convinced he was a Detroit Lion scout.

Then, too, Billy never has forgotten the famous saying of that old Chinese coach named Confucius: "Coach who win game seldom lose friend."

O'Brien, a leader among Chesapeake Democrats, has a winning record that most politicians would envy. In the last nine years—the 1960s—he has averaged about one defeat per season. Of course, one loss can ruin a politician but in football campaigns one defeat out of 10 tries is not bad.

The O'Brien record since 1960 is 71 victories, 11 losses and eight ties. Over-all the Wildcats under O'Brien are 103-28-9.

In tenure as head coach, Billy is the No. 1 man in the Southeastern and Eastern Districts. Ralph Gahagan of Wilson has more years as a head coach but some of his service was outside of Tidewater.

As the dean of Tidewater coaches, O'Brien has a thousand memories. He recalls what a reporter said to him on the sideline as Great Bridge played Newport News with the state championship at stake about six years ago.

Reflection at Beach Training Camp

"There were only seconds to play and was 7-7," O'Brien remembers. 'We had a firs down on their one-yard-line. We didn't hav any more timeouts but for some reason New port News called time. I called my quarterbac over and told him exactly what to do. All of sudden this writer rushes over to me and say 'Coach, this is a pretty big play, isn't it?' "

As you may have guessed the Wildca goofed on the big play, the score remained 7- and the state title was lost. Needless to say the reporter is no longer in sports.

O'Brien will never forget the stormy nigh another Peninsula eleven — Warwick — wa leading an unbeaten Great Bridge team whe lightning struck the field and knocked out th power. To O'Brien the hero on that occasio was the late Doug Eley, then the Great Bridg principal.

"All the lights were out and it was so dar you couldn't see your hand in front of you face. There was a high fence between us an the stands and I figured that Doug was up i the press box. We were standing around on th field not knowing what to do.

"I don't know how he climbed that fenc or how he even found us in the pitch black dar but I know Doug ran up to me and said, 'Ge the team together and get on the bus. We'r going back to Great Bridge.' "

Score one for the incomparable Mr. Eley The game was called, Great Bridge went hom and returned the following Monday night, onl this time the Wildcats went home a winner.

"And then there was the time . . ."—Hol it, coach, save some of the memories for you 20th year. Let's get on with No. 15.

COACH O'BRIEN

By RUSSELL BORJES
Virginian-Pilot Sports Writer

My wife says this picture of Billy O'Brien makes him resemble Ronald Reagan. I disagree with my wife but I must hasten to add that, like most wives, she usually is right.

Since the theme for this year's program is the 1968 political conventions and ensuing presidential election, it was natural to pose Coach O'Brien as a delegate delivering an address. If he winds up looking like a national political figure, I figure I'm ahead of the game.

Of course, it is not surprising that O'Brien should look like a politician. He was Chesapeake campaign manager for a successful candidate who is now in the Virginia General Assembly. He recently was a delegate to the Virginia Democratic Convention.

Since 1955 the 39-year-old head coach has been engaged in winning football games at Great Bridge.

Publication of this program originated in 1960. Since that time Wildcat elevens under O'Brien have lost nine games in eight seasons. In four of the last six years his teams have been undefeated, the longest such streak reaching 27 games.

The record in the 1960s is 64 victories, nine defeats and seven ties.

A football coach does not stand on his past record, however. That is why O'Brien has been working perhaps a little harder this season.

"Bill's doing the best job he's ever done in football," Blevins says. "He has more organization now and he's handling the offense himself.

For Coach O'Brien there is a new job this year, too. He has become Supervisor of Physical Education for the Chesapeake secondary schools.

The new position will take him away from Great Bridge each morning. It may eventually take him away from his first love — coaching football. O'Brien doesn't like to discuss the possibility but this may be his last year in coaching.

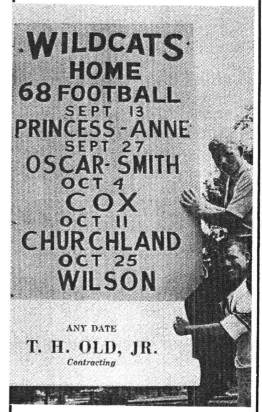

Overtime Work Pays Off for O'Brien

By RUSSELL BORJES
Virginian-Pilot Staff Writer

Billy O'Brien worked overtime last week. Besides his daily duties as coordinator of driver education in Chesapeake schools, he supervised installation of new driving simulators which arrived last week.

The simulators were purchased with part of a federal grant of $136,000 to Chesapeake schools which O'Brien was instrumental in securing for the education of student driver trainees.

Because he has a wife and two children, O'Brien recognizes the importance of proper training for future motorists. Thus, he has thrust himself into the driver training program, which is new for him, with his usual diligence.

Oh, yes. Last week O'Brien, who also coaches the Great Bridge football team, found time to lead his Wildcats to perhaps their greatest victory—a 31-24 triumph over a Wilson team that observers had called the best scholastic eleven ever assembled in Tidewater.

Believe it or not, O'Brien actually missed most of one practice last week and was hard-pressed to make several others.

When he took his Wildcats over to Portsmouth last Friday night, they were anywhere from 12- to 20-point underdogs.

If the game provided Great Bridge with its greatest victory—and O'Brien says it was—it also was one of the greatest scholastic contests ever played in this area.

"After the game," says O'Brien, "Bill Story came up to me and said it was the best game he'd ever seen between two high schools. If Bill Story, one of my idols when I was in high school, thinks that, who am I to disagree with him."

Story, a veteran educator, coached some of the greatest scholastic teams in Tidewater history when he was at Granby in the 1940s.

Both coaches—O'Brien and Wilson's Ralph Gahagan—had their squads well-prepared for the showdown between unbeaten, untied teams, both of which ranked in the top five among Virginia teams.

Neither team seemed to be able to stop the other's offense, which led to the excitement of high scoring. Great Bridge led, 23-8, at one point but the Portsmouth Presidents overcame that 15-point deficit and went ahead, 24-23, in the final quarter.

Then Wilson made what turned out to be two fatal mistakes.

Great Bridge, with a fourth and short yardage situation, went into punt formation close to midfield. Wilson, thinking the Wildcats were faking the punt, did not send back a punt returner. The Wildcats did kick, however, and the ball was downed at the Wilson three yard line.

Wilson couldn't maneuver offensively that close to its goal and was forced to punt. The kick was short and Great Bridge got the ball at the Wilson 17. The Wildcats scored, then time ran out on a desperation Wilson drive and Wilson had suffered its first loss in 21 games, including a 40-0 rout of

O'Brien: Administrator at work

Great Bridge a year ago.

Great Bridge, which never has had a perfect season, is 6-0 and must be given an excellent chance to finally win a state championship, which always has managed to elude the Wildcats despite several unbeaten seasons.

Of course, O'Brien realizes that 6-0 is not 10-0 and four more games, including the Homecoming contest with Deep Creek tonight, must be won if his dream is to come true this year.

One thing that most people seem to have overlooked is that Great Bridge has played five of its first six games away from home.

This is a genuine homecoming for the team as well as the alumni. There have been four consecutive away games. The Wildcat faithful—who more than did their share in filling up Lawrence Stadium in Portsmouth last Friday—will be able to stay at their Hall Stadium and find out whether this will really be THE year.

The last four games will be played right here, including what may develop into the game to decide the state title—Norview vs. Great Bridge here on Thanksgiving morning.

O'Brien, remembering that some of his better teams of the 1960s have been denied state crowns because of one slip during the year, is keeping his fingers crossed.

The coordinator of driver training for Chesapeake is hoping to coordinate this latest drive of his football team to the ultimate destination—No. 1 in the state and the state title before 1970.

I wish I had made fun of Billy during one of his early years as Great Bridge coach by telling him "Yeah, you'll win a state championship the year they put a man on the moon." Wouldn't I have looked like a prophet now?

✓ New Era Starts Tonight for Wildcats

By RUSSELL BORJES
Virginian-Pilot Sports Writer

One of the most sensible maxims in sports is that you do not break up a winning combination. This has been the No. 1 coaching principle for Billy O'Brien at Great Bridge over the past four football seasons.

Playing the percentages, taking few chances on fumbles and controlling the ball did not always win full support of the fans but the system won 33 games out of a possible 40 with only two defeats on the record.

But there is another maxim that O'Brien is fully aware of—what you did yesterday does not always win games today.

Two consecutive defeats this season have driven that point home with emphasis. So O'Brien is doing what seems to come naturally with him. He's changing his philosophy, his system and his coaching staff to fit his personnel.

It may come as a surprise to some people that O'Brien is able to throw out all his old theories and begin anew. He has been pictured as a stubborn conservative who refuses to take chances regardless of the situation. Stories in this program have tended to create such an image.

This reporter was purposely exaggerating the characterization in search of humor. But no matter how you approach them, two straight losses are not funny, especially when they come on the heels of a 20-game unbeaten streak.

Coach O'Brien has taken and passed the test of change before. When he first came to Great Bridge he installed the split-T offense even though he knew little about the formation. In his second season he moved his offensive backs into the line on defense and started the first of his unbeaten streaks.

When Great Bridge grew into a Group One school, O'Brien was using a wide open attack featuring Linky Pratt, pitchouts and frequent passing. But the coach realized that most of the Eastern District schools outweighed and outnumbered Great Bridge.

He searched for a new formation that would allow him to combine two-on-one blocking and deception. He found such an offense in the winged-T. Great Bridge was the first district eleven to perfect the winged-T attack.

It was such a perfected offense that rolled up the highest number of points among State Group One teams in 1960. O'Brien seldom practiced defense because he was confident his offense could shake a back or two loose for long touchdown runs every game. The Wildcats won eight straight games, including a 38-18 victory over Cradock, before losing to Maury in the mud.

The 8-1-1 record of 1960 was duplicated in 1961 with an improving defense. Then came the two unbeaten years of 1962 and 1963. This was the era of Buster O'Brien and Charlie Carr at Princess Anne. But during this period Princess Anne was never able to beat Great Bridge.

Coach O'Brien began an intensive scouting program with Princess Anne as the subject. In 1962 Great Bridge used 32 different defensive alignments against Princess Anne and held the O'Brien-Carr passing combination scoreless. Great Bridge learned PA's plays so well that O'Brien actually installed some of them in his own offense.

Last year Princess Anne had perhaps the best material developed at a district high school in years. On paper the Cavaliers were superior to the Wildcats but the Wildcats won, 20-7.

If you were coaching at Great Bridge and had not lost in 20 games, would you have broken up the winning combination? O'Brien's answer was to continue using what had been winning.

So far this year, however, the speedy back who can break open a game with a quick touchdown has not come forward. But O'Brien does not blame the players. He blames O'Brien. He believes it is the task of the coach to suit the offense and defense to the available personnel. It is easy to win, he feels, if you have the best material. Winning regardless of the material is the true test of a coach's ability.

"After the Princess Anne game," says O'Brien, "I felt bad because I thought the boys had let me down. After the Cradock game I felt worse because I knew I'd let the boys down."

(See page 13)

O'BRIEN PASSES BUT BATHING SUITS FLUNK
By RUSSELL BORJES,
Virginian-Pilot Sports Writer

Don't let those occasional passes and trick plays fool you—Great Bridge coach Billy O'Brien is still a dedicated conservative.

He votes the straight Darrell Royal ticket. Royal, the University of Texas coach, is known as the Barry Goldwater of college football.

Royal is said to be so conservative that he looks both ways before crossing a one-way street. O'Brien probably looks both ways and then decides not to cross.

O'Brien is so conservative that he refused to allow the cheerleaders to pose for program pictures in bathing suits. "You know, most of them wear two-piece suits," he exclaimed. You'd think two-piece suits had been outlawed.

The conservative outlook of Coach O'Brien extends into the off-season. This past summer he worked on his master's degree in physical education at the University of Virginia. He's taking no chances on the future.

If he has a couple of bad seasons he can always become a principal like most of the ex-coaches in the Eastern District.

So far, however, he hasn't had to worry about losing his job. He went into the current season with only two defeats on his record in the past four years.

He hadn't lost in 20 games when the 1964 season opened.

As a scholar he has also compiled an excellent record. He received A's on both subjects he studied during summer classes.

O'Brien's conservatism is reflected even in the new uniforms worn by the Wildcats this season. Billy says they are copies of Chicago Bear uniforms. The Bears are probably the most conservative team in pro football.

It's a wonder that O'Brien decided to use the Bear-type uniforms—they are two-piece suits.

Conservative, liberal, reactionary or radical, you can't argue with the success of the University of Texas, the

Chicago Bears—or the Great Bridge Wildcats.

Texas was the nation's No. 1 team last year, the Bears won the National Football League title and Great Bridge went 8–0–2.

Two-piece bathing suits may be banned but watch out for O'Brien's naked reverse. It's a honey.

P.S. Coach O'Brien's ulcer is doing fine, thank you, but the conversation he and photographer Lonnie Johnson had when they were going to set up the picture above was a little sick.

"I've had mine a little over a year," said O'Brien with what seemed to be a touch of pride.

"That's nothing," said Johnson, "I'd had mine for years and years. You're just a rookie." Johnson appeared to be boasting about his old ulcer the way my old Army sergeant used to brag about his being in more chow lines than I'd been in pay lines.

They can keep their ulcers and the sergeant can keep his chow lines, too.

Two Decades with Coach O'Brien
146 Wins 43 Losses 11 Ties

Two decades have come and gone since the tall, lanky Marine Captain with the crew cut came on the scene as the Great Bridge Football Coach. There were no shopping centers or housing developments in Great Bridge then, just a few houses and the parking lot behind the stadium was a cornfield and no one really cared whether the bridge was open or closed.

Since that time, Great Bridge Football Teams have become synonymous with the words, "they play good football out there," and his teams widely acclaimed by the citizens of Tidewater and all over the state.

The 45-year-old former University of North Carolina end, who has developed Great Bridge into one of the top teams in Virginia, didn't realize he had seen 19 teams come and go until reminded recently.

"It can't be that many" he said; counting the years on his fingers. "It seems like just yesterday. . . ."

Some of the youthful exuberance may be gone, but Billy still retains a remarkable power of concentration for his favorite sport. If you don't believe he is always thinking football, try to talk to him about something else during a practice session.

And if he fails to recognize you when you pass him on the street or in the halls of the school, it's not that he is impolite. He is simply figuring how to get that linebacker to commit himself an the off-tackle play—or how to explain to his wife that he won't be home because of a junior varsity game.

Despite his seeming aloofness, O'Brien hasn't lost many friends during his 19 years at Great Bridge. One of the reasons is that he is a friendly, fun loving person during the off-season. You should have seen his performance at a Baltimore Colt Game about two years ago. He had 10 Colt fans convinced he was a Detroit Lion Scout.

Then too, Billy never has forgotten the famous saying of that old Chinese coach named Confucius: "Coach who win game seldom lose friend."

In the recent general assembly election, Billy was elected to represent the people of Virginia Beach, Chesapeake and Portsmouth in the House of Delegates. He won the

Election by over 12,000 votes.

During his recent stay in Richmond, O'Brien gained much respect from his fellow representatives for his ability to work hard and long and is one of the best liked new representatives.

He was recently selected to represent the State of Virginia in a meeting with members of the Texas Legislature and other Southern States in San Antonio, Texas to discuss problems of mutual concern.

When asked if his new job interferes with his coaching, he replied, "There are so many areas that I now have to be knowledgeable about that I sometimes wonder whether I will someday have to terminate a career that I have lived my whole life to do, because I cannot tolerate failure."

Staff Photos by Charles Meads

Rain Sends Team Indoors

Kenny Whitley, a Great Bridge Jayvee Candidate, Watches Rain Pouring off the Classroom Roof at Camp.

Football Goes Military in Camp

By DAVE LEWIS

VIRGINIA BEACH—The head coach is the commanding officer, his assistants as sergeants and the players are raw recruits. This is how the Great Bridge high football machine operates on maneuvers at Camp Farrar.

Billy O'Brien's Wildcats began their fifth straight year at Camp Farrar this week where discipline, spirit and togetherness is the watchword and finding a winning formula is a must.

One can't argue with success. O'Brien has sent his forces through four summer camps and has only suffered two setbacks in 40 games.

* * *

"The most important thing we gain at these camps is morale," said O'Brien as he patiently waited for the thundershowers to stop yesterday. "These boy have a lot of pride."

Camp Farrar, covered wit pine needles and sand, is just living and sleeping quarters fc Great Bridge. The Wildcats combat two miles away on practice field at Fort Story.

"We had a boy killed comin to practice in 1959," recalle O'Brien. "It was then I decide a camp like this would be idea But I never dreamed of the a vantages it would bring."

* * *

Camp Farrar is equipped wit small cabins for sleeping qua ters, a mess hall, an infirmar showers and a large classroon for meetings.

The day usually begins at 6:3 a.m. although 5 a.m. is mon likely if humid weather is for cast. Clean-up details, bed-mal ing and inspections give th camp a military splendor.

"Everybody has a job," sai O'Brien.

"We have two practices, tw meetings and no one is allowe to leave the cabins during th rest period. Lights out are usua ly at 9:30 and anyone caugl AWOL is off the team."

* * *

"I always looked forward camp," said Raleigh Voight, former Great Bridge star wl is helping the Wildcat coachir staff before going to Virgir Tech next week.

"It's not all work. We alway had a lot of fun pulling pranl and fooling the coaches. You learn about the guys you pla with by just living next to the for a week."

While it rained, O'Brien her ed his Cats into the classroo and showed them last year

Staff photos by Charles Meads, *Virginian Pilot.*

Resting for Another Practice

In Left Bunk, Robert Wilson (Bottom) and George Schucker Join Allen Hall (Bottom) and Danny Carpenter in a Mandatory Rest Period.

A Helping Hand

Billy Field (Right) Helps John Hall With His Shoulder Pads For Meeting and Light Workout.

Staff photos by Charles Meads, *Virginian Pilot.*

Billy O'Brien, Forgetful Genius

By RUSSELL BORJES

Virginian-Pilot Sports Writer

Since losses are blamed on the head coach, so too should credit for success go to him. Coach Billy O'Brien has provided Great Bridge High with its greatest football hours.

In 1957 his Wildcats won the District One, Group Two title—the first in the school's history. Last year—only three seasons after joining the Eastern District, Group One conference—O'Brien's eleven became the newest State power.

The 1960 Wildcats won eight straight games, were ranked No. 1 in the State most of the season, and held district champion Norview to a 0-0 tie in a memorable Thanksgiving Day game.

Great Bridge fans still consider that deadlock a major moral victory. And who can blame them? Norview at that time had played 36 games without defeat and it was the first time in six years the Pilots had been held scoreless.

O'Brien began coaching while he was still starring in football and basketball at Wilson High in the late 1940's. (And all the rumors about him leaving Great Bridge for Wilson were false. The truth is that he and his wife Joyce are building a home in Wilson Heights —in Great Bridge.)

Billy gave up coaching the Park View midgets to attend North Carolina. He was a regular End in his sophomore year and played on a Cotton Bowl team. In his last five years as head coach—he is in his seventh season—O'Brien has won 52, lost 15 and tied three.

Although O'Brien is regarded by his colleagues as one of the best young coaches in Virginia, he sometimes concentrates on football so much that he forgets everything else. Last Thanksgiving after the Norview game

he didn't even know what day it was.

This is in the nature of a warning about him and his team. You never know what will happen next—and the surprises don't stop with the lightning-like touchdown bolts on the field. He often puts wild ideas into practice, like the current system he uses for calling plays.

You have to watch O'Brien every minute. One of these nights he'll forget his pants. Watch him closely.

Staff photos by Lonney Johnson, *Virginian Pilot.*

The Virginian-Pilot
November 16, 1969
O'Brien Voted Prep Coach of the Year
By Dave Lewis

Billy O'Brien of Great Bridge, who led the Wildcats to the Southeastern District championship with a 10-0 record and a berth in the Eastern Regional Playoffs, today was voted high school football Coach of the Year.

The poll, conducted by the *Ledger-Star*, has O'Brien a runaway winner with 78 votes. Of 25 ballots sent to area coaches, 18 were returned with O'Brien a solid winner.

Based on a 5-3-1 point system, O'Brien outscored Bob Tata of Norview 78 to 23. Ralph Gahagan of Wilson, who won the award last year, was third with 14 points.

The Wildcats finished the regular season 10-0 and met Hampton in the Regionals with a State Group I-A championship at stake. However, Hampton prevailed last weekend 42-0.

O'Brien who finished his 15th year as head coach at Great Bridge, has produced nothing but winning teams since the Wildcats entered the Group I-A ranks. He has had five unbeaten seasons, 9-0-1 in 1962; 8-0-2 in 1963; 9-0-1 in 1965; 10-0 in 1966 and 10-0 this year.

"It's a team effort," said O'Brien. "I could have never done it without my assistant coaches."

O'Brien's assistants are Jimmy Calhoun, Cecil Jennings, Martin Oliver, Bob Broda and Tony Zontini. Calhoun has been on O'Brien's team for the last 12 years.

The veteran coach also gave credit to Great Bridge principal Harry Blevins, who was once one of the most able assistants.

"It can't be done by one individual," said O'Brien. "Lora Hinton can't run without blocking...although he sometimes does it. It's a team effort."

O'Brien realizes the impact coaching has on football players. He fondly remembers his own high school coach, the late Dick Esleeck of Wilson.

"I guess I would have been a bum if it wasn't for Coach Esleeck," said O'Brien.

"In my freshman year at Wilson I skipped school 38 days. One day Coach Esleeck came up to me and said, 'Hey boy, you stay in school from now on.'"

"Coaches do have an influence."

O'Brien played on Wilson's 1947 State championship team under Esleeck and went on to play for the University of North Carolina.

"Coaching is what I've wanted to do since I was 15 years old," said O'Brien.

He wanted to return to Wilson to coach but was turned down so he went to Great Bridge, then in Group II, and has built a powerhouse throughout the 1960s.

And he has made Wilson remember its mistake. He holds a 4-1-1 edge over the Presidents which includes a 31-24 victory over the favored Presidents this year. Wilson went on to a 9-1 season but finished second to O'Brien's Wildcats.

"It's been a good life," said O'Brien, who has compiled a 113-29-9 overall record at Great Bridge. "My wife has had to put up with me too."

O'Brien received 15 of 18 first place votes. Other first place votes went to Tata, Bert Harrell of Lake Taylor and Jim Henderson of Indian River.

O'Brien was left off entirely on two ballots.

Tata, who led the Pilots to an Eastern District championship with an 8-2 record, was a solid second choice.

He said earlier that O'Brien should be Coach of the Year just on his win over Wilson.

Tom Rogers of Granby, who had a 7-3 record in his rookie year, finished behind Gahagan with 12 points.

Next were Harrell with eight points and Henderson and Charlie Wade of Cradock tied with six. Others receiving votes were Royce Jones of Norfolk Academy, Jerry Sazio of Maury, Bill Ralph of Kellam, Johnny Palmer of Hampton and Charlie Nuttycombe of Newport News.

She'll be Cheering Team and the Coach
Ledger-Star, Wednesday, December 3, 1969
By BETH HURDLE

CHESAPEAKE—Joyce O'Brien has her heart set on a Wildcat victory Friday. And she'll be cheering both the team and the coach.

Victory would mean the first state championship for her husband, J.W. (Bill) O'Brien, during his 15 years of coaching football at Great Bridge High.

"There have been other times—when we have had undefeated seasons—that I thought we should have been state champions," the coach's wife said.

The Wildcats, already Southeastern District football champs, will put their 10–0 record on the line Friday evening at Foreman Field when they play the Hampton Crabbers, Virginia's only other undefeated team this year.

Joyce's cheers might not be quite as loud as they were Thanksgiving Day, when the Wildcats defeated Norview, because she hasn't regained the full volume of her voice yet. But she's a sure bet to be in the bleachers watching every play.

Football is ever-present in the O'Briens' Wilson Heights home this time of year.

Friday nights she's at the games. Saturday she gets to review the movies of Friday night's game. Then it's college and professional football on TV.

Even at the office she doesn't escape the football talk. Being the coach's wife and the secretary (and only woman) in the Process Engineering Department at Ford's Norfolk Assembly Plant, Joyce hears lots of "if they had done this" about the games.

"I do begin to feel fully saturated with football. When it's over, we begin a new way of life," she said.

But toward the end of the summer Joyce is apt to show up at football camp at the beach. Nor is she a stranger at practice sessions and the first scrimmages of the new football seasons.

Fifteen-year-old son Joe is the family's football player, but he hasn't seen too much action this year.

"Joe broke his leg the second day of practice. His was the first injury of the season," his mother added.

"He's really more of a basketball player. Joe is already 6 feet 2 1/2 inches tall," she reported.

Like her mother, 10-year-old Marlene is sports-minded. Her goal is to be a varsity cheerleader.

A native of Murfreesboro, N.C., Joyce attended Chowan College.

She first heard of Bill O'Brien when he played end for the North Carolina Tar Heels.

"I saw him play, but I didn't know him then," she said.

The couple met in Portsmouth.

"Actually we met when he was in the Marine Corps. He was standing on the corner talking with some of my friends—probably watching the girls go by—and that's exactly what I did—go by."

A native of Kansas and graduate of UNC at Chapel Hill, O'Brien is the son of Mrs. J.W. O'Brien of Conway, Mo., and the late Mr. O'Brien.

"Portsmouth had been Bill's home since first grade," she said.

Joyce made the move to Portsmouth with her family also. Her mother, Mrs. Mary McLawhorn, resides in Portsmouth. Joyce is the daughter of the late Ned Joyner.

Although she can't report on her husband's grid-iron days, Joyce does recall the early coaching days.

In order to insure a long winning streak, O'Brien wore the same coat, trousers and tie to each game.

"It really upset me to think that everybody would think he had nothing more to wear. But he wore the game outfit the rest of the season."

The game outfit custom has been put aside by the coach, but the coach's wife hasn't altogether curbed her sideline coaching tendencies, she says.

COACHES' SALARY DISCREPANCY

The City of South Norfolk and Norfolk County had merged, forming the City of Chesapeake. This was accomplished to prevent the Cities of Portsmouth and Norfolk from annexing certain tax providing areas from Norfolk County. Ed Brickel was superintendent of South Norfolk Schools and Ed Chittum was superintendent of Norfolk County Schools. Both of these men were well educated and very intelligent. They were deeply involved in politics. Some considered them as the actual political bosses of their respective governments. My problem was that Superintendent Brickel paid his coaches double the amount as the Norfolk County coaches were receiving. This came to light while I was attending an Eastern District Coaches' Association meeting in 1966. It was a business meeting for all the coaches in the area.

During a break, one of the South Norfolk coaches asked me how much I was getting paid for coaching football. I said, "Six hundred dollars a year." That was probably about ten cents an hour for a football season.

He was surprised. "I'm making twelve hundred dollars a year," he said.

We were now in the same school system. Yet for the same job he was earning twice as much as I. At first I felt exasperated, then sad, and later vengeful. After this experience, I realized how many things in our lives are political.

At a meeting later with just the Chesapeake coaches, I told them of the pay difference. It was hard for them to believe what they were hearing. The entire group were shocked, upset, and mad as hell. The next day I called our Superintendent Chittum and said that I wanted to meet with him to discuss coaches' salaries.

I went to his office in the school administration building. It was a fine building that had been built to his specifications. When I confronted him about the salary problem, he didn't really have an excuse. He told me that everyone was still under the original contract as before the merger and would stay the same for the time being. He said that adjustments would be made in the coming year to make it fair.

The next year two separate contracts were issued; one for teaching and one for coaching. Everyone was paid the same amount for coaching. It was a small victory, but I had little consolation for the being underpaid for over ten years. Ultimately I would seek some kind of consolation in politics and work for better salaries for all teachers and coaches.

Here's the reason for the problem in the first place. Mr. Chittum was appointed by the school board. The school board was appointed by the County Board of Supervisors. Most of the supervisors were good, honest farmers who relied on Mr. Chittum for guidance and advice. He was a smart man who wanted to keep his job. He wanted to keep the cost of education as low as possible. If you keep the teachers' salaries down, there's no need to raise taxes. No tax hikes would enhance his job security. Politics controlled not only salaries but also controlled what you taught and how you taught it. Politics controls every facet of public education.

After finding out about the salary differential, I realized that if I wanted to shape my own destiny and help my fellow teachers and coaches have a living wage, I'd have to eventually become a politician. At the time, I wasn't even a registered voter. I was a coach, a good citizen, and a high school teacher. I had no idea that I'd one day play a decisive role in some major issues as a member of the House of Delegates, but the motivation to do that was now in place.

RUNNING A CAMPAIGN FOR NED CATON

In the fall of 1966, six months after I had confronted Superintendent Chittum about salaries for coaches, I was approached by Rhae Adams and Roger Malbon to be a campaign manager for Ned Caton.

Rhae was the owner of a Ford dealership in Virginia Beach and a political guru. We had grown up together in Portsmouth and were good friends. We had paper routes delivering the *Virginian Pilot* from 4:00 to 6:00 a.m. during World War II. We sold extra editions when Germany surrendered in 1945 outside the Park View gate of the Portsmouth Naval Hospital.

Roger Malbon was a successful businessman in Virginia Beach. He enjoyed politics and sports. He served as chairman of the Virginia Beach Democratic Party. Later, Roger became a political advocate for me and a great lifetime friend.

Four candidates were running for three seats in the Virginia State Senate. My candidate, Ned Caton, was the underdog by a long shot. His primary opponent in Virginia Beach was Bill Kellam. His father was Sidney Kellam, who ran all the politics in Virginia Beach.

Other candidates included Bill Hodges of Chesapeake and William Moody of Portsmouth. Everyone from the cities of Portsmouth, Virginia Beach, and Chesapeake were to vote for three representatives to the Senate. Any of the other three could be edged out by Caton. He was an underdog candidate and supposed to lose Chesapeake by three thousand votes, but with a winning coach running his campaign, there was a chance.

At first I wasn't sure that I wanted the job. On one hand, I thought it might be a way to get back at Mr. Chittum for using politics to underpay coaches so he could keep his job. On the other hand, I had never done any political work, had no idea what was expected of me, or how much time it would take.

My first duty was to read a speech to the press. Rhae Adams wrote the speech for me about why it would be great to elect Ned Caton. I read it before TV cameras and reporters from three television stations but asked them not to question me about anything after I read the statement.

The evening after the speech had been aired on the nightly news, I was at a softball game at Great Bridge and people began asking where I was going to work next year. At first I had no idea what they were talking about. They said, "Don't you know that every elected official in Chesapeake is for Bill Kellam."

By running a campaign against Kellam, I was campaigning against every city official. That included the board of supervisors who appointed the school board. I thought to myself, *I knew Rhae Adams had not told me everything.*

I went hone and told my wife about the problem and she said, "You had better call everybody you know in all three cities." That's what I did. I stayed on the phone for about a month. Having played on the 1947 state champion high school football team to crowds in Portsmouth of nearly thirty thousand people, I was well known there. My Great Bridge teams were winning ninety percent of their games. The fans were most loyal and enthusiastic. The entire community supported the team; so asking for their support of Ned Caton was received more favorably.

When I called people, I said, "Hello, this is Billy O'Brien. " They would say, "Hey Coach, how are you doing?" I'd say, "I need your support of Ned Caton. He's a good man. Please vote for him and tell all your friends to vote for him."

Ned Caton was supposed to lose by three thousand votes in Chesapeake, but won by fifteen hundred votes. He carried the entire district and won the seat.

As a result of this victory, I gained fame in politics overnight. When I had the opportunity to run for the House of Delegates in 1973, I knew the fundamentals of the election process and campaigning.

Eighteen Years of Friday Night Lights

After my first winning season (second year of coaching), we never experienced a losing season. It has been said that "little things mean a lot." Here are some of the little things that I did to fulfill my dream as a coach and at the same time created the Great Bridge pride in the hearts and minds of the players.

My main objective in life was to produce wining football teams. Everything else except my family was secondary.

I coached track to produce fast backs and fast ends. I coached state champions in the hurdles and tackles and guards who won state championships in the shot put and discus. I did not cheat and practice football in the off season. I coached wrestling to have the guards, tackles, and backs be agile, quick, and strong and to develop the courage and mental capacity to take on anything that confronted them. I checked on their grades and their schedules to make sure they had the correct courses they needed to go to college. Teachers loved to have my football players in their classes because they knew if the boys did not behave, they would not play ball for Coach O'Brien. I spent twenty years of my life producing football players to win on and off the field.

The first things I did when I got the coaching and teaching job at Great Bridge was to procure a movie camera to film games and to install face masks on every helmet.

Knowing the importance of game films, somehow I had to obtain a camera so I could analyze our games. I went to our principal and asked if we might purchase a camera. He told me there was no money for a camera. I suggested that we hold a school dance and charge the students a quarter for attending. We made fifty-three dollars, and off to a pawn shop I went to purchased an 8mm camera.

When I was playing football at the University of North Carolina, my nose was broken twice and many of my teammates had their front teeth knocked out. If you received a cut on your face during the game, a doctor would put stitches to mend the cut right on the field as you sat on the bench. That way the player could go back into the game. A few players did have face masks but they were just for someone with a broken jaw or other injury.

If a player received a facial cut when I was coaching, I would not send him to a general practitioner to sew up the cut. I made sure that the player went to a plastic surgeon. I had an agreement with a plastic surgeon to treat my players.

When playing at UNC, we had a trainer, Fritz Lutz, who would not allow players to drink water before or during the game. That's hard to believe, but that is the truth. It is a wonder that he didn't kill someone. His theory was that water clogs the muscles and you would be able to react more quickly if the muscles contained no water. It is difficult to believe that a university such as UNC allowed such a thing.

Later I learned how harmful and dangerous it was to deprive athletes of water. We always had water breaks during practice sessions, and water was always on the bench for our games.

During my entire football playing career, I never was allowed to lift weights. There was a belief that by lifting weights you would bulk up your muscles and become slow and uncoordinated. Paul Dietzel, head football coach at LSU, wrote a book about weight workouts. After reading it, I had the first weight room and weight program for football players. We lifted in season and off season.

Many knee and ankle injuries are not caused by being hit by another player but because cleats from their shoes get caught in the grass and the knee or ankle is injured. To prevent this from occurring in practice, we had the players practice in tennis shoes that had little rubber cleats and did not easily get caught in the grass. We used regular football shoes during our games.

When we practiced for teams, we would have all of the drills done off of our game field. When we had eleven against eleven on offense and eleven against eleven on defense, we would use our game field. Defense would be at one end of the field and offense at the other end, and we would change the end of the field every other day. This is called extrasensory perception and this does give you great home field advantage.

Our staff would scout our own team about twice a year. We lost a state championship because Newport News found a procedural defect that our fullback was doing. We were running the wing-T formation and our fullback ran the ball on four different trap plays. Coach Charlie Nuttycomb of Newport News High School discovered that when our fullback ran a trap play, he dropped his right foot back into a sprinter's position. If he ran the fullback belly series or any other play, he would line up in a balanced stance. During that game our fullback was stopped and just about everything else we did was stopped because they knew what we were going to run by the fullback's stance. We did tie the game 7–7 and finished the year with a 9–0–1 record. However, Danville High School finished 10–0 and won the Virginia

State Football Championship. That's when I instituted the "scout your own team" at least twice a year.

This same young fullback scored five touchdowns on traps in one game when we beat Norview 35–0. This is an indication of his talent when the opposing team did not know to watch his foot placement.

We were playing Deep Creek at their field. I sent my wingback into the game to tell the quarterback to call a screen right. One of the Deep Creek chain holders heard me and immediately started yelling "screen right" to the Deep Creek defensive team. I called time out so I could talk to the referees about moving their "chain gang" to their side of the field. They refused the request, saying that it was against the rules.

After the incident at Deep Creek, I had men, not high school students, working the first-down yard markers. When these men were working the chains on the opposition's side and they heard anything the opposing coaches said, they informed me by little hand signals.

These next two events may seem bizarre, but they happened to me twice. Always striving to have winning seasons, I paid a lot of attention to details.

We would have our manager bring a tape measurer to all away games for measuring hash mark distances and the extra-point line distance.

Coach Larry Weldon of Craddock High School, who was a former Washington Redskins quarterback, would spread his wide receivers and backs all over the field. After one game in which they beat us, I was looking at the game film and was sure that his hash marks were wrong. The next day I went to their stadium and measured them. They were two and one half yards less than they should have been. I never told anyone, but I would show the referees when we went there to play.

Another team we played in Portsmouth liked to run for two points after a touchdown. I took a tape and measured the extra-point line. It was a foot and one-half short. Again I only spoke to the referees when we played them on their field.

In 1965 I went to Atlantic City, New, Jersey, to attend a football coaching clinic for high school and college coaches. The clinic was held in the auditorium where Miss America was selected. There were about five hundred coaches in attendance. Coach Vince Lombardi of the Green Bay Packers was one of the speakers. He was diagramming the Green Bay sweep when he paused for a moment and pointed to a particular booth and said, "There is the best coaching aid that I have ever used, and I suggest, after I complete my lecture, that you take a look."

When he finished all five hundred coaches tried to get to that booth. When I finally inched my way there, I saw for the first time a VHS camera and TV video. Both were inherently large in comparison with the present ones. The price for the unit was an astonishing three thousand dollars.

After returning home, a meeting was arranged to request buying one of the units for my use. After explaining to Doug Eley why I wanted it, he said, "How much does it cost" When I replied three thousand dollars, he said, "O'Brien, you are crazy, no." After much discussion and persuasion, I had the first VHS camera in Virginia.

The next season we began using our equipment. We would set it up on our sideline and would film the defense in one series. When they came off the field, we would put the tape in the TV and the defensive coach would point out what the players were doing wrong. The camera filmed the offense when the defense was off the field with the same procedure occurring.

Before playing Oscar Smith, we were informed that we would not be allowed to use their electrical outlets for the VCR equipment. I rented a gas generator. We beat them and used our VHS also.

I used the machine to coach the track team during practice sessions as well as track meets.

The following year, the Virginia High School League passed a rule banning the use of the equipment in football games. So there I was with a three thousand dollar machine that I couldn't use.

I read an article in a coaching magazine that players actually use the food that they consume on Thursday in the game on Friday night. When I was at UNC the football team was fed at 10:00 a.m. The meal consisted of a T-bone steak, baked potato with no butter, a tossed salad with no dressing, and a small glass of orange juice. This was the worst pre-game meal before an afternoon game.

The article said that a player should digest large amounts of pasta, potatoes, and fruits to overload the body with carbohydrates that would eventually be stored in the liver as glycogen and would be released as glucose when the muscles needed the food to perform the blocking, tackling, and running to play the game of football.

I persuaded the school cafeteria to serve spaghetti for lunch on Thursdays for the carbohydrates the team would need. I even had a few of my players over for dinner at my house. My wife would cook a meal high in carbohydrates.

I had a bad experience when two players came to play a game after they had left school and drank a few beers. I dismissed them from the team and put into place a rule that all players report to the stadium immediately after the last period on a game day. We watched football films and served them a meal consisting of a can of nutriment that served as a meal for people trying to lose weight. The players hated it.

After using the nutriment for some time, I noticed that we were not having muscle cramps. Later I read that muscle cramps are caused when muscles lack calcium, and the nutriment contained a large amount of calcium. I had always been taught that the lack of salt caused cramps and there-

Coach Billy O'Brien, John Rollinson, Charles Olah, fullback, Eastern Division Champions. Photo by Lonney Johnson, *Virginian Pilot*.

after I stopped forcing my players to take salt tablets.

I had a great friend in Great Bridge, W.A. "Dick" Davis. Dick was the announcer at all of our home games for years until one Friday night he got a little carried away when Linky Pratt broke down the sideline for a sixty-yard touchdown. In his excitement he said, "He's on the fifty, the forty, the thirty. Look at that little son of a bitch run." Very soon after that incident, our superintendent told our principal that he would have to fire Dick. That was his last game announcing.

We were still real good friends, and Dick so wanted to be a part of the team. This time I created a job for him by placing him in charge of keeping unauthorized people out of the press box. We were playing Woodrow Wilson from Portsmouth, at home. Mike Alford, superintendent of Portsmouth Schools, wanted to sit in the press box. Dick, being so zealous about his new responsibility, told him that he could not sit in the press box. After the game, he called our superintendent, Ed Chittum, and Dick had to be dismissed from that job.

Not giving up, we found another job for Dick. He was put in charge of keeping people out of our locker room after the game. Coaches should not allow anyone except sportswriters in their locker room. If you allow parents or fans to come in you are just asking for problems. Anxiety can be very high right after a game.

For two years Dick performed this job with diligence until one night after a loss. Lt. George Paspas of the Chesapeake Police Department, who had a son playing on the team, wanted to come in. Dick refused and Lieutenant Paspas knocked Dick on his butt. That led to the termination of that job. He and Doug Eley had been good friends for a very long time, but there would be no more assignments. The two of them began watching the games in the opposing team's press box, which was not in use.

When I was elected to the House of Delegates in 1973, I hired Dick as my legislative assistant. He worked in that position for two years and did a great job. At the end of the second session, Dick had a heart attack and died. It was one of the saddest days of my life when we laid him to rest. I lost a great friend and someone who was like a second father to me.

For years we had an annual game with Norview High School on Thanksgiving morning, and it was always a complete sellout. We would have crowds of twelve thousand people at every Thanksgiving morning game for ten years. It was not only attended by the Great Bridge community but also by others who just wanted to see a good high school game. It became a tradition that was looked forward to by all football fans.

When the Virginia High League decided to have state playoffs to determine a state champion, we had to stop playing on Thanksgiving Day because it would interfere with the playoff schedule.

Great Bridge football had the most loyal and devoted fans. The Wildcats seemed to be the heart and soul of the community. We sold three thousand reserve seat tickets before the season even began. Robert Cooke, a neighbor who was the proprietor of Cooke's Hardware in Great Bridge, sold these tickets for fifteen years.

The receipts from our football teams financed the entire athletic program with the exception of the basketball team that took care of their own financial needs. Today most programs are financed by the school board at the taxpayers' expense.

When I resigned from coaching in 1974, Great Bridge High School had one hundred fifty thousand dollars from the profits of our football games. The money was in a financial institution accumulating interest.

During the twenty years of "Friday Night Lights" walking the sidelines, we had a four and six record my first year coaching and the following nineteen years were winning seasons. My last year of coaching our team record was five wins and five losses. At that time I was a member of the House of Delegates.

I came to the realization that I could not do both jobs at the same time. I could not politic, legislate, and coach football. This would be unfair to my players. I resigned as football coach of Great Bridge High School.

O'Brien: 146–43–11 Record
Scholastic 'Knute Rockne' Honored
By JACK ARMISTEAD, October 21, 1975
The Virginian Pilot

CHESAPEAKE—The monstrous task of contacting every football player who played under former Great Bridge High School coach Billy O'Brien is now being made.

O'Brien stepped down from coaching at Great Bridge this year after a brilliant 20-year career.

Wayne Head and Ken Barefoot, two former Great Bridge football players, are trying to round up the "O'Brien Army" in order to honor their former coach at a testimonial dinner which has been scheduled for December 5 at the Moose Lodge on George Washington Highway.

Head and Barefoot have asked all former O'Brien-coached football players to contact them at 499-6821 or 499-6881 so that arrangements can be made to make the event a memorable one.

Head said time is running out for contacting the more than 500 players involved.

O'Brien, the "Knute Rockne" of high school football in Tidewater, compiled a career coaching record of 146–43–11.

Head said the purpose of the event is to show O'Brien that two generations of former football players at Great Bridge are grateful for the dedication he displayed.

"We are expecting a good turnout," said Head.

The main problem, Head pointed out, is getting all the replies in by December 5.

O'Brien is a member of the legislature in addition to currently being administrative assistant to the principal at the Chesapeake Center for Alternative Rehabilitative Education.

Looking back on some of the highlights of his career coaching at Great Bridge, O'Brien cited "the first time we beat Churchland" when he began coaching as one of the most memorable.

"My first year Churchland beat us 60–0," said O'Brien.

But in his second year, Great Bridge snapped a nine-game losing streak to Churchland by beating the Truckers 14–0.

"If we hadn't beat them the second year, I think I would have ended my career right then," said O'Brien.

Then O'Brien's teams went on to defeat Churchland 19 out of 20 times.

Another highlight?

"Deep Creek just beat us once in 20 years," said O'Brien.

"I never cut a kid that came out," said O'Brien, adding that once in awhile a kid was forced off the team due to disciplinary action.

"It was a very, very enjoyable career. I miss it on Friday nights. I miss the real close rapport with the kids, "said O'Brien.

And vice versa.

Calling all O'Brien players....

Coach Billy O'Brien and wife, Joyce. Photo by Lonney Johnson, *Virginian Pilot*.

Running for the House of Delegates

I ran for the House of Delegates in 1973 when a new seat was created by the federal government.

The federal government had created three floater seats, which were for Northern Virginia, Richmond, and Tidewater. The Tidewater seat consisted of the cities of Portsmouth, Virginia Beach, and Chesapeake. Those sections of the state had not had representation in keeping with their population. Southwest Virginia had previously run the state even though they had a smaller population. They were also much more conservative than the northern and coastal areas.

I saw the announcement of the new seats in the paper and decided to run for the Tidewater seat. I wanted to play a part in making laws because of the inequity in teacher's salaries.

I had grown up in Portsmouth where I was still well known from my athletic high school and college days. Many of the Portsmouth people continued to follow my career.

My family and I had lived in Great Bridge for nineteen years. The football team was winning about 85 percent of their games and was the pride of our community. The other Chesapeake communities—Deep Creek, Churchland, Western Branch, Oscar Smith, and Indian River—were envious of the winning seasons our football team produced. We were respected for our sportsmanship and spirit of the team, students, and fans.

Even though I wasn't as well known in Virginia Beach as in Chesapeake and Portsmouth, there was some name recognition. Some of the identity probably came from coaching track and football against their teams and earlier by actively taking part in their politics.

The first thing that I did was go before the Chesapeake School Board: I requested a leave of absence for the time when the General Assembly would be in session. I told them, "I need this leave when I win the seat in the House of Delegates."

They all started laughing. "Sure, O'Brien. We'll let you have a leave of absence if you win." Then they laughed some more. I was a coach going up to Richmond where the legislature was run by 75 percent lawyers. It was big joke.

The next thing I did was call Roger Malbon, one of the two guys who had recruited me to campaign for Ned Caton. Malbon owned a successful trucking company and loved politics and sports. He had a bookie and bet on every college and pro football game that was played each year. He was a tall, big guy, who was generous, kind hearted, and had a wonderful personality. Roger was well known and respected throughout the Tidewater area. He came from a family of pig farmers and made it in the big city. He was in his sixties. I was forty-four years old and had been coaching and teaching for nineteen years.

Malbon replied, "Sure. I'd love to." He didn't like Bev Middleton, who I was running against. Middleton was really a pretty nice guy. He had already served in the House of Delegates for ten years, representing Virginia Beach. He decided to run for the floater seat because he thought that if he won, he'd have it forever.

It was a three-month summer campaign to win the Democratic primary. Whoever won the primary would be elected in the general election since there wasn't an active Republican party to submit a candidate.

Fortunately I had the summer off from teaching and was working part time in the Department of Recreation.

I had aggressive campaign organizations in Portsmouth and Chesapeake, and I was on the phone calling everyone I knew, just as I'd done for Caton six years earlier. Between my efforts and Malbon's enthusiasm, I won the election in July 1973 by twelve thousand votes—the largest margin in the history of the House of Delegates.

I was the second high school teacher ever to get elected to the General Assembly.

MY FRESHMAN YEAR IN THE HOUSE OF DELEGATES

I had never been to the Virginia Capitol in Richmond until I won the election. In early January, 1974, Joyce and I, with Roger and Clara Malbon, drove to Richmond. I had been requested to come to the Capitol as a part of the freshmen orientation.

As we got closer I saw the impressive, towering gray-white dome of the oldest existing state capitol building in the New World. Roger had stopped the car at the foot of the long drive leading to the Capitol. After saying good-bye to them, I walked a few steps, turned and waved again. At that moment, I felt as if it was my first day of school. I wondered if it might be like boot camp in the Marine Corps.

When I approached the guard building, a capital policeman came to me and said, "Do you need some help?" "Yes sir. I just got elected to this place. Where do I go?" He replied, "Come with me and I'll show you." He gave me a thorough tour of building.

The next day I was assigned a legislative office that was about the size of a small bathroom. It had two chairs and a desk with a window overlooking Broad Street. There was one secretary who worked with three other delegates. I was assigned a seat in the chamber.

I went to the Holiday Inn on Franklin Street to make arrangements for a room while the General Assembly was in session. Most of the delegates and senators stayed there as it was convenient to the capitol. I later learned where some of the state's legislation was passed—in the bar at the Holiday Inn over a couple of drinks.

The freshman delegates went through about four days of orientation. It was like a high school government class. We practiced the procedures that we would use on the house floor and in the committees. We learned to address the speaker of the house as "Mister Speaker." I would say, "Mister Speaker." He would say, "The gentleman from Chesapeake."

We received a directory of all of the members of the House and Senate. I took that back to the Holiday Inn at night and tried to memorize every person's name and what they looked like. At that time ninety-five percent of the house and senate members were Democrats. That was the heyday of the Byrd organization.

Harry Byrd was a United States Senator from southwest Virginia, who had been the controlling figure in Virginia politics. At that time he was in full control of the state. It was like Tammany Hall in New York. I was not aware of it, but you were supposed to ask his permission to even run for office. Henry Howell, the former lieutenant governor, had a great deal to do with the demise of the Byrd organization.

My first bill was related to an alcohol beverage control law. Before I arrived at the House of Delegates, a bill had been passed to lower the beer-drinking age to eighteen. It was felt that if lads were being drafted to serve in Vietnam, they were old enough to buy beer. There were many students in high school who were eighteen years of age, but very few who were nineteen.

I had heard of numerous problems this was causing at high school dances and school functions, so I introduced a bill to raise the drinking age to nineteen. That's when I got my first taste of lobbying and special interests. Miller, Budweiser, all the beer companys' lobbyists went after me like a herd of buffalo. They wanted to stampede me into keeping the age limit as it was so they could sell more beer.

I found out more than I wanted to know about lobbying. The lobbyist contacted all of the legislators who had gotten campaign contributions from the beer industry. The bill was killed.

One thing that I learned was, before you enter any legislation, you had better do some research to find out who you're going up against and how valid the principle of the bill really is. People were always calling me with ideas for bills, and I had to determine if a bill was valid.

I was assigned to the Education Committee and to an Interstate Cooperation Committee that never met in Richmond. It was a committee that met in other Southern states with other Southern legislators.

The Interstate Cooperation Committee creates compacts between states to achieve a common goal. For example, you can't have too much of a difference between states over hunting and fishing laws. It was from this committee that I eventually got the idea for the lottery.

Some of the big committees included Appropriations, Finance, Education, Insurance, Banking and Corporations, and General Laws.

Freshman delegates, generally didn't get major committee assignments. I sought all the help I could get for an assignment on the Education Committee, and I got it. I wanted to do what I could for teachers and students.

My Sophomore Year in the House of Delegates

Before my second year in the House of Delegates began, I did some research and found out that sixteen-year-old drivers were involved in 30 percent of all accidents in our state, yet they made up only five percent of the people driving cars. Insurance rates were raised accordingly for families with young drivers.

The most important thing in a teenager's life is obtaining a driver's license. At one time, I was the driver's education coordinator at Great Bridge. Working with the student drivers and the instructors, I became aware of the significance the teenagers placed on being able to drive. They derive a huge amount of freedom and independence from their parents. I was going against the grain when I introduced a bill that would require the minimum age a person would be licensed to be raised from sixteen to eighteen. I thought it would help increase safety on the roads.

When word of the bill got out, I felt like the building had fallen over on me. It made headlines all over the state. The legislators killed the bill so quickly it made my eyes blink. Fellow legislators, as well as myself, were receiving calls and letters from students, parents, and car dealers to kill the bill. I could not imagine what an impact it made on the public. The bill had a very short life, as it was killed in the first committee meeting.

As a member of the Interstate Cooperation Committee, I went to a Southern Energy Board meeting in Knoxville, Tennessee. Several companies in Tennessee, which made radioactive materials used in the treatment of cancer, went bankrupt and left barrels of radioactive material in store rooms unattended. The barrels rusted and radioactive material leaked into rivers and contaminated water supply systems in small towns.

I recommended that a bill be introduced so that this would never happen in Virginia. It required that a company producing radioactive materials would have to properly dispose of the waste. Any company that manufactured materials such as those had to be bonded so that, if the company went into bankruptcy, there would be money to pay for the cleanup.

I had the bill drafted by Legislative Services and I introduced the bill. A few days later I met with Jerry Baliles, who was in the House of Delegates and later became our governor in the late eighties. He was a lawyer and had been involved in some litigation involving just this sort of problem. He asked me to let him handle the bill. I said, "That's fine, but I've introduced it already and it's under my name." He suggested that we change the name on the bill but, I told him I'd rather keep it as it is.

The bill did get through the house and over to the Senate. There was a little trouble with Senator Ed Willey, who wanted to know how much it would cost the state. I said, "Little or nothing." Later I found out that it did cost a lot because the companies had to be monitored.

That was my first bill to become the law of the state. It went into the Code of Virginia.

Street Lights

My son, Joseph William O'Brien III, was the second leading scorer in high school basketball, averaging 26.8 his senior year at Great Bridge High School. He was talking to me about the difference between mercury vapor and high-pressure sodium light bulbs. He said that Virginia Power Company, or VEPCO, was using mercury vapor bulbs in all the street lights in Virginia cities and towns. He also told me that all of the federal military camps and bases were using high-pressure sodium bulbs for their illumination needs. The difference between these two bulbs astounded me. The mercury vapor light uses twice as much electricity and gives less illumination than the high-pressure sodium bulbs. *That's when I saw the light!*

I had Legislative Services prepare a bill that, in essence, required VEPCO to replace all mercury vapor bulbs with high-pressure sodium bulbs in Virginia. VEPCO is a private company which rewards its stockholders depending primarily on how much electricity it sells to its customers.

No sooner had I introduced the bill to the docket when I went to my legislative office and was met by five officials of VEPCO. They were led by Bill Crump, lobbyist for the company, who went by the nickname of "Ready Kilowatt."

When I entered my office, he greeted me by saying, "What in the hell are you doing introducing this bill? You will bankrupt VEPCO." He went into a tirade explaining how much it would cost his company. I told them to get the hell out of my office because I was elected to protect the people of my district and of my state, and I was doing what I was elected to do.

The group left my office in a huff, but the next day they had a proposition for me as to what they would do if I withdrew the bill. They said that they would replace every mercury light with a high-pressure bulb as it burned out. I really did not want to get into a big fight with VEPCO, and this seemed a way to accomplish what the bill would do. I agreed to withdraw the bill on the condition that they send me a monthly report on how many bulbs were replaced. They said they would do this.

I can say that all street lights in Virginia are high-pressure sodium bulbs. That's those orange-colored bulbs you see when riding down the streets at night.

University License Plates

In 1987 a suggestion from my daughter, Marlene Castellow, caused me to introduce a bill that ended up bringing in millions of dollars to colleges in Virginia. After she graduated cum laude from Virginia Tech, she and her husband moved to West Palm Beach, Florida. While my wife and I were visiting them, she said, "Wouldn't it be great if Virginia had license plates with the names of colleges on them like they do here in Florida?"

I thought it was a goad idea and introduced a bill to that effect in the next session of the House of Delegates. The passing of this legislation will be an insight on the behind-the-scenes give and take in politics.

My bill easily went through the House, but it had to pass the Senate. It was there that the bill ran into opposition from Senator Hunter Andrews of Hampton, the second most powerful man in the Senate.

Andrews had a bill which accelerated the collection of sales tax on all businesses in the state. I always believed in helping businesses because if you're good to business, people will be working and taxes will be paid, and some of that tax money will go to teachers. I voted against his bill, and, as a result, he killed my license plate bill.

During the session the following year, I voted for a bill that Andrews wanted to see passed, and now my bill passed both the House and the Senate.

Even bigger problems started. I got a call from Josh Darden, the son of former governor Colgate Darden and a ranking member of the Board of Visitors at the University of Virginia. He said, "I like your license plate bill, but we want some of the money. Unless every college gets to collect $15 of the $25 cost when those plates are issued, we won't sell the plates."

This meant that I had to change the language of the bill to accommodate the demands of the colleges. When I went to discuss this with the Speaker of the House, A.L. Phillpot, there was a big problem. He was a devoted University of Richmond alumnus, which is a private university that received very little money from the State of Virginia. He said to me, "Instead of giving money to a rich school like the University of Virginia, I want all the revenues from those plates to go to the Department of Motor Vehicles."

Speaker Phillpot was going to kill the revised bill. I thought, *Down for the count again.* I decided to wait and address the changes to the bill in the next year's session.

The next year, I got a break when Bill Lemmon, the chairman of the Education Committee, retired. Since I was the most senior member of that committee, I automatically became chairman. That meant I ran the whole show for education for the Commonwealth of Virginia. The superintendents of schools all over the state shivered. Coach Billy O'Brien was now Mr. Chairman of the Education Committee. They knew that I was going to be on the side of the teachers.

The Virginia Education Association, an organization of teachers, had about five lobbyists in the state legislature. They were delighted as I was a member of their association and a friend of the teachers.

After becoming chairman, I talked to every legislator who had introduced bills that would come before my committee. The chairman of a committee has the absolute right to present the bills before his committee members as he chooses. If I wanted to, I could decide not to put a bill on the agenda, and thus it would languish forever.

Because they knew that I had this power, everyone voted for the bill with the changes I wanted—money to go to the colleges.

Ultimately the sale of the plates for worthy causes brings in millions in revenues for a variety of organizations, including schools, environmental causes, the performing arts, and others. We are now the number one state in per capita income from these license plates. The only state that surpasses us in total revenue is California, which has a lot more people than Virginia.

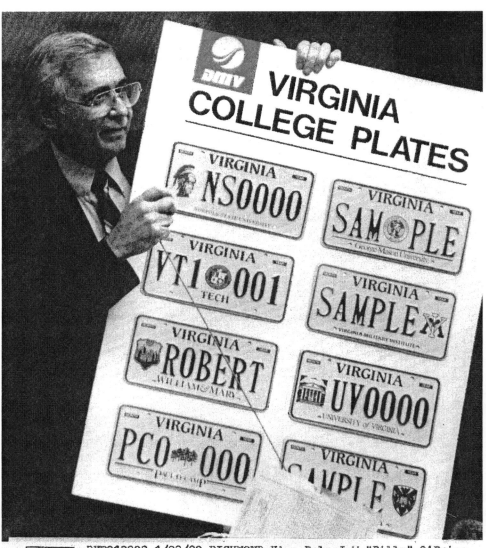

RVP012202-1/22/90-RICHMOND,VA.: Del. J.W."Billy" O'Brien
(D-Va. Beach) holds a display of license plates with sym-
bols of state colleges and universities in the House of
Delegates 1/22. O'Brien sponsors a bill that would funnel
scholarship money to the schools from plate sales.
UPIu   jm/ Joe Mahoney

RVP020602-2/6/87-RICHMOND, VA.: Del. J.W. "Billy" O'Brien, D-Va. Beach, displays a prototype license plate bearing the insignia of a state university, this one being James Madison University, O'Brien has introduced legislation that would allow the sale of plates with other schools emblems to motorists who want everyone to know their alma mater. UPI jm/Joe 'ahoney

Del. O'Brien Is In Line to Head Panel
By THOMAS BOYER, Staff Writer
The Virginian Pilot

VIRGINIA BEACH—Del. J.W. "Billy" O'Brien, one of the first educators in the General Assembly when he took office 11 years ago, is now in line to be the next chairman of the House Education Committee.

O'Brien, a Virginia Beach Democrat who was a near-legendary football coach before he entered politics, was third in seniority among Democrats on the committee this year. The chairman, Dorothy S. McDiarmid of Vienna, is expected to move on to head the Appropriations Committee.

That leaves only Alan A. Diamonstein of Newport News, who is not expected to leave his post as head of the powerful General Laws Committee and would not chair two committees at once.

"I won't take anything for granted until I see the committee assignments," said O'Brien, 56. He represents the 83rd District, which includes the Bayside area.

If all goes as expected, he will become chairman of a committee that has influence in a wide range of education policy, from naming state-supported colleges to discipline and personnel practices in local school districts.

He acknowledged that the committee is not considered as powerful, even in education matters, as the House Appropriations and the Senate Finance committees, which ultimately control the amount of money the state spends for schools.

"The big game is in appropriations," O'Brien said. "We have to pass [education bills], but then they go upstairs to get funded."

Nevertheless, the Education Committee is one of the crucial places for hammering out the state Standards of Quality, the regulations all local school divisions have to obey. The standards, which have been significantly changed in recent years are part of an education reform movement, are up for revisions again next year.

O'Brien said he has no changes in mind for the committee, saying he would continue to run it the way it was run by McDiarmid.

While he remains an educator—as a counselor in the Chesapeake schools—he has kept his distance from Virginia

Education Association, the statewide teachers' organization.

"I don't think I've represented any special-interest groups," he said. "I've been against collective bargaining and really didn't get a lot of financial support from the teachers because of that."

An official of a teachers organization, who spoke on the condition he not be named, said: "He can be really tough on us."

O'Brien is, however, responsible for introducing the state requirement that local school boards adopt their budgets in the spring, before teachers leave for summer vacation.

Teachers' organizations were assured that their rank and file would be available to lobby school boards at budget time, and O'Brien says the rule is "the most important piece of legislation ever passed in the state of Virginia, as far as teacher salaries."

In House votes in 1985, he supported the VEA position twice, voting for bills to give teachers a voice in local student discipline policy and school curriculum.

O'Brien also opposed two VEA-supported bills that won legislative approval. They raised the age for entering kindergarten and required tougher inspections for asbestos in public buildings.

Whoever ends up chairman, O'Brien expects the education committee soon will face two big issues: changes in the state subsidy formula for local schools, and a proposal to expand the minimum high school day from six periods to seven.

The subsidy formula is now under study by a joint House-Senate committee. O'Brien said the committee's report may suggest changes in the formula that mainly would benefit urban school divisions with large low-income populations. He said he would oppose any changes that would steer funds away from Virginia Beach.

But O'Brien favors expanding the number of periods in the day. Recent expansions of the state graduation requirements, to 22 credits, have meant that many students have been unable to fit such electives as band and vocational programs into their schedules.

Rather than let elective courses fold, he said, he would support either lengthening the high school day—a change that would also undoubtedly involve teachers' salaries—or shortening class periods.

"Whether I'm chairman or whoever's chairman, we're probably going to have to go to a seven-period day," he said.

The committee post is likely to boost the political stature of O'Brien, who rated 50th out of 100 members of the House of Delegates in a survey of legislators, lobbyists and reporters conducted in January by *The Virginian-Pilot* and *The Ledger-Star*.

In that survey, O'Brien's rating was not as high as his seniority. He is tied for 27th in House seniority—23rd among the Democrats in control.

He discounted the rating, saying the results were skewed by lobbyists who dislike him.

O'Brien is known statewide for his unflagging—and unsuccessful—push for a state lottery, which he has advocated for four years.

The easygoing former Great Bridge High School football coach acknowledges that he has had more success getting his teams to score touchdowns than he has had in convincing the General Assembly to pass his bills.

In the 1985 session, O'Brien sponsored five bills. Four never made it out of House committees; a fifth—establishing a pilot program for so-called "latchkey children" in Virginia Beach—passed the House, but died in the Senate Finance Committee.

From the House of Delegates on the License Plate Bill

Mr. O'Brien: The purpose of this bill is because of the fact that some of the colleges of the state and the Division of Motor Vehicles felt that if the alumni of some of the colleges were going to use these plates, they felt that they should be entitled to some of the money. And experience in other states has been that the states where colleges do receive some of this money for scholarships a lot more plates are sold. For example, in the State of Florida, they sold 80,000 plates and in the State of Georgia 29,000 plates have been sold for the University of Georgia. In Pennsylvania where they don't have this capability, they haven't sold that many plates. What this bill does is allow, after a college sells 1,000 of these plates, the college will receive $15.00 of that plate money of $25.00 and it will be placed in the State Treasurer and later on, the Council of Higher Education will monitor the money and they will allow these colleges to use this for scholarships for in-state students only. And in this state, ladies and gentlemen, some of you may have seen it over in the House floor but right now we have 36 institutions in this state and one institution, Penn State University, by the way, Penn State has sold the most plates. But, the provisions of this bill, they will receive none of this scholarship money. It's just in-state colleges and for in-state students. Hopefully, we will report the bill.

Del. George Allen: The provisions for this fund would be for those who are Virginians and also that are enrolled in educational programs other than those providing religious training or theological education. That, gentlemen, is pretty obvious that you're trying to do there but isn't that exclusionary discrimination so to speak. There is discrimination that's constitutional and unconstitutional. Has the Attorney General's Office made any comment as to whether it's constitutional to treat religious studies at our colleges and higher institutions differently than poetry classes or history courses or whatever.

Warren Stanbaugh: Mr. Speaker, ladies and gentlemen of the House, I hope you will defeat this amendment. Perhaps the language is not artfully worded and some people have suggested that it may tend to disqualify somebody who was in a biology program and happened to take a competitive religion course or something. I don't read that language as doing that but I can understand that somebody has that concern. But that certainly is a minor kind of language change that would give the Senate something to deal with what they so desperately need. Mr. Speaker, what really concerns me is taking out this entire language because then what you are doing precisely what our Constitution I believe prohibits is you are directly paying a student to receive religious education, training to be a minister or a priest or a rabbi, and I think that is promotion of religion and I think that it is prohibited under our Constitution and this bill will be struck down at the very first chance it ever got to court and I don't think the gentleman from Virginia Beach wants to lose this bill that way. And I hope that you would defeat this amendment.

George Allen: Speaking of the amendment, Mr. Speaker, as the gentleman from Virginia Beach says we do have a tuition assistance draft which goes out directly to students and they may take religious training, they may take theology courses, whether it is in Buddhism or various religions we may have around the world or some that may be defunct as well but some folks they want to bring back. At any rate, the Constitution Section 16 of Article 1 hits this matter in this regard it says that "persons shall not be compelled to frequent or support any religious work or place of ministry whatsoever." Now the argument generally adapts by the gentleman from Arlington. However, it goes on to say "nor shall these people be enforced, restrained, or molested burdened in his body or goods nor shall otherwise suffer on account of his religious opinions or beliefs. But all men shall be free to profess it and by argument to maintain their opinion in matters of religion" and here's the key point "and the same shall in no ways diminish, enlarge, or effect their civil capacity." Now, in the event a student wanted to take religious training as opposed to poetry or some other sort of a course by the largesse of the languages that this amendment compounds, they would not be able to get some loan assistance. It's a tough situation here that we're trying to balance, but in my view, in view of the fact that we do have theology courses in private colleges and state colleges. We have tuition assistance, grants in private colleges, we pay for buildings, we pay for facility in private, excuse me, in state colleges. It seems to me that we should not burden or restrain people who want to take these courses. And in the event there is another sort of language that the Senate may come up with which tightens this better. I think that the preferable thing would be to adopt the floor amendment and pass it on fairly constitutional measures. I would say to the gentleman, that in the event that a state college whether it's the University of Virginia or Virginia State or VCU or Tech or any other have religious training or theological education courses, we'd already be violating his constitutional concern because we are to some degree assisting our state colleges of higher education. If they have a theology course there already, obviously in the budget, the gentleman from Henrico would agree that there is sufficient funds going to our state colleges. So you can say even having that course, find out why this would be unconstitutional. Secondly, I'm not certain that they actually have courses, or state colleges provide religious training. However, they may have theological education in that you may have theology courses, you may have comparative religion courses, you may have various religious courses but it is important to understand the religion of some countries, understand its history and its future and its present goals. So, in my view, if they are giving it to religious studies even through this funding mechanism, they already have then in existence it would be unconstitutional what they are doing now. But, in fact, I don't think that they have too many of those sort of courses, if any now, but they certainly do have something which would come under the parameters of these words "theological education" which would then preclude such a student who is taking a theology course possibly from getting this assistance whereas one who is taking regular non-theological courses could get that assistance.

Warren Stanbaugh: Mr. Speaker, I hate to get into a religious argument on this license plate bill but I think you have to know what's going on. The gentleman from Albemarle is absolutely correct in one thing he said. If you are going to an institution that has religious training, that is training to be a minister as I read the language of this as I tell you, is not precisely drawn but I think that's the intent. And you are going to that same university and training in biochemistry then as the bill now stands a biochemistry student would be eligible to get a scholarship from this money and the student studying for the ministry would not be. And it is discrimination. And it's exactly the point of our constitutional provision in Article 1, Section 17, and the First Amendment of the United States Constitution is that we don't use state money to pay people to study to be ministers. That's as much for the protection of those who are studying to be ministers as it is for the state because you know and I know that once the state gets into that, then the state can start controlling things. The public funds, Mr. Speaker, let me say to the gentleman, they are public funds when they are collected and the fact that they are distributed to somebody else doesn't make them any less public funds, Mr. Speaker. And I think that's a very important point to know the structure of what happens here. This is not like a grant where the money is given directly to the student and the student goes off and does heaven knows what with them. And I don't know about tag grants and I'm not an expert on those. Just tell me what I understand. That they are given to the student and the student uses them as he or she pleases. And they are not loans which the Supreme Court says it's all right to give loans to people who are going to a religious institution because those are paid back. But our Supreme Court says and I have not read the tape because I didn't think we were going to get into this debate but just reading the notes here in the code, it is said as long ago as those in 1965 that if you spend state money to authorize payment of tuition and other expenses to people going to sectarian, that is religious kind of schools, that violates that part of the constitution. And when you give money to an institution and it gives scholarships to pay tuition and other expenses, that's the same as I'm saying that our Supreme Court over 35 years ago said was unconstitutional. And I would say to the gentleman from Virginia Beach, this bill if it were to pass like this, would meet the same fate, I believe. And as laudable as it may be, the thing we want to help people study religion and I don't want to help some people any more than anybody else, it is interference, it's direct interference with taxpayer money into religion and I think it is unconstitutional and I hope you will reject this amendment.

Clinton Miller: Mr. Speaker, ladies and gentlemen of the House, regardless of the constitutional provisions in the debate we just had, this bill adds another provision to the special license plate legislation. Now, remember when the special license plates were first enacted to just a few, one section then two and three. We kept on adding all these things. It's an egotistical trip for a lot of people to have special license plates to say this or that. The justification for this bill to set up a special scholarship fund in this convoluted fashion is carrying to extreme the provision of the special license plates. I can't imagine that the University of Virginia, as I've heard, has indicated that their people won't participate in an ego license program unless they get something special out of the fund. Now, the general provisions of this law provides that all of these fees collected, every license fee collected under this ego tag concept, goes into the General Fund to meet the expenses of the Department of Motor Vehicles. That's in the first section of this article. All the money is supposed to go in there to meet the expenses of the Department of Motor Vehicles. Now, if you do this, let me predict what is going to happen. If people, in order to get the ego tag, you're going to have to get more out of it other than just the ego trip and get some money coming back to their special interest, then you're going to have other people coming forward and saying, why can't we get a portion of that special license fee back to support, perhaps volunteer rescue squads or volunteer fire companies, perhaps programs for the handicapped, perhaps programs for the Veterans of Pearl Harbor. I sense I'm losing this argument. But now put prevality aside, you are setting up a special dispensation of these funds within this chapter when all the other provisions for these ego tags put the money back into the department for operations and for what they call the expenses of the department. I think this is a bad concept to do this and the way it's being done to set up this special scholarship arrangement is also inherently bad. I tend to vote against the bill.

O'Brien: Mr. Speaker, ladies and gentlemen of the House. What harm can this bill do? It is a simple measure that allows the alumni to show pride in their alma mater. It makes a valuable contribution to the scholarship fund at no cost to the Commonwealth. And, in fact, my bill should be viewed as a way to help my friends and colleagues on the Appropriations Committee for additional revenues for the colleges and universities. We set aside on our tax forms in the Commonwealth a place for all Virginians to contribute to the welfare of birds and bees. And this bill will let them contribute to the welfare of the three R's. And just this morning I passed a display right in our building and I saw a picture of the rotunda of the University of Virginia and I say to you, ladies and gentlemen, that Thomas Jefferson would support this bill. I saw the Spartan of Norfolk State and this bill would help to provide additional scholarships for deserving minority students. I saw the Lion at Old Dominion and the Monarchs would take great pride in this bill. The proud eagle of Mary Washington College will raise its wings on its license plate and it would help Mary Washington rise to greater heights and don't forget Virginia Tech. This bill holds the Hokies high. And as for VMI, this bill stands like a stone wall. Hope it will be the pleasure of the House to vote in favor of the bill.

Clinton Miller: Mr. Speaker, of course, ladies and gentlemen of the House, we all recognize these first bills that come on the floor for debate get much more debate than they merit and with all due respect to the gentleman from Virginia Beach, I appreciate his comments and I'm sure there is a goodly number and probably a goodly majority number here on the floor of the house that will help this fine gentleman reach his meritorious goal of whatever it is he is trying to achieve by this bill. But I just want to remind you in all seriousness the precedence you are setting again. These kind of measures were not in the inception intended to be measures to raise funds for any of these groups that are covered by these kind of tags. All of these funds are supposed to go back into the Department of Motor Vehicles for operating costs and once you set this precedence, you're going to have not only those in the future who are going to be coming here for special tags wanting to share in the revenue thereof as a condition for participating in the program but you're going to have the people who are already covered coming back and wanting to get a piece of the pie. I think it's bad precedence to set. It wasn't intended for that purpose and we shouldn't include that in the code. And I can't imagine that all the vast alumni of that great institution in

Charlottesville that if you went to them, regardless of participation in this program if they would say that this is a condition. That we've got to get something in our hands to participate. The largest participant in this program, Penn State University, isn't going to get any benefits from this because they are an out-of-state college. But just think of the precedence you're setting. I'm telling you that if you're going to allow the University of Virginia and these colleges to set up scholarship programs through this, it's no less meritorious than to have training programs for various entities that want special tags in the future. And for that reason, I believe the bill should be defeated.

Mr. Speaker: I's 52, no's 42, the bill is passed.

Funds Disbursed to Institutions Participating in the State License Plate Program

	1992	1993	1994	1995	1996	1997	1998	1999	2000	2001	2002	Total
College of William & Mary	$1,635	$5,520	$9,930	$9,840	$10,005	$11,805	$12,930	$15,960	$20,595	$22,110	$24,075	$144,405
Emory & Henry College								$1,770	$2,955	$3,285	$4,035	$12,045
George Mason University						$1,920	$2,385	$3,185	$5,355	$6,480	$7,620	$26,945
Hampden Sydney College									$3,450	$4,455	$4,620	$12,525
James Madison University	$8,925	$5,040	$8,925	$11,115	$10,080	$10,245	$10,395	$12,105	$16,890	$19,500	$21,885	$135,105
Longwood University									$2,415	$4,875	$5,655	$12,945
Mary Washington College								$1,365	$3,240	$3,750	$4,185	$12,540
Norfolk State University									$3,240	$4,755	$6,015	$14,010
Old Dominion University					$1,395	$2,730	$3,195	$3,975	$6,450	$7,650	$9,285	$34,680
Radford University						$1,380	$2,940	$4,140	$6,900	$8,205	$9,000	$32,565
University of Richmond			$1,035	$4,320	$4,290	$5,115	$5,505	$5,970	$7,605	$8,325	$8,970	$51,135
University of Virginia	$5,355	$6,660	$12,420	$10,650	$11,265	$18,405	$26,325	$32,280	$45,165	$53,655	$60,420	$282,600
Virginia Commonwealth Univ.							$360	$2,250	$3,345	$7,935	$9,255	$23,145
Virginia Military Institute			$3,675	$6,000	$6,840	$6,480	$7,755	$8,910	$10,675	$11,805	$13,125	$75,265
Virginia State University										$2,130	$4,230	$6,360
Virginia Tech	$22,635	$15,495	$39,405	$31,380	$30,540	$32,865	$47,940	$60,315	$95,385	$123,870	$137,490	$637,320
Washington & Lee University									$930	$2,505	$2,805	$6,240
	$38,550	$32,715	$75,390	$73,305	$74,415	$90,945	$119,730	$152,225	$233,665	$292,785	$329,865	$1,513,590

Artistic Licenses? Va. Gives the Old College Try
Vehicles Could Have Any U.S. School Logo
By Donald P. Baker, *Washington Post* Staff Writer

RICHMOND, Feb. 13—The Virginia General Assembly is going to give motorists a chance to exhibit the old School Spirit.

A bill headed for passage would permit the bureau of motor vehicles to design and manufacture a special license plate bearing the logo of any college in the United States.

Several other special plate bills are also working their way through the General Assembly, including special plates for survivors of the Japanese attack on Pearl Harbor on Dec. 7, 1941, and another for recipients of the Purple Heart.

The sponsor of the college logo plate legislation is Del. J.W. (Billy) O'Brien (D-University of North Carolina, University of Virginia), who admits that he is "always looking for ways to raise money without raising taxes."

He originally proposed limiting the plates to Virginia colleges, but members of the House of Delegates, many of whom who are graduates of out-of-state institutions, amended the bill to include their various alma maters.

One change extended the plates to all states contiguous to Virginia, another to selected colleges around the country, and Del. David G. Brickley (D-Penn State) tacked on states that are part of "the Chesapeake Bay basin," to include Pennsylvania.

There are "8,000 rabid Penn State fans" in Virginia who would pay good money to display a Nittany Lion on their license plates" argued Brickley, as he held up a tattered Penn State athletic jacket.

Before the debate got out of hand, Speaker A.L. Philpott (D-University of Richmond) gaveled the old grads to order, and parochialism was set aside in favor of an all-inclusive resolution.

The bill, which is to come up for a vote in the Senate next week, gives the commissioner of motor vehicles the authority to manufacture a batch of college plates, as long as there are enough potential buyers. A minimum of about 300 is needed to cover the cost of casting a special die. Each plate would cost an extra $25.

Since they were introduced in 1981, special-order plates have become so popular that between 10 percent and 12 percent of all automobiles registered in Virginia already carry them, producing more than $4 million in income for the state. Most of the tags cost an extra $10. Virginia is one of the top three states in the percentage of cars with custom-ordered plates.

In addition to the proposed Purple Heart and Pearl Harbor plates, a special plate has been proposed for survivors of the Battle of Chosin Reservoir in the Korean War. Another proposal would extend the right to an existing special plate for former prisoners of war to include civilian nurses who were captured.

Not a college graduate? Not a war hero? Virginia still may have a special plate for you.

There are already special plates for Medal of Honor winners (eight have been issued) and members of the American Legion; Civil Air Patrol; Chamber of Commerce; Coast Guard, National Guard, Army, Navy, Air Force and Marine Corps reserves; fire departments; rescue squads; disabled veterans; (regular) veterans; pharmacists; judges; ham radio operators; honorary consuls; drivers of cars more than 25 years old (divided among antique, hobbyists and street rods), and for pool vehicles.

All of those are in addition to people who qualify as handicapped or hearing impaired, and, of course, members of the House of Delegates, state Senate and Congress.

Still don't qualify? Buy a Great Seal plate for a one-time extra fee of $25, as 20,000 Virginians already have, or any of the remaining combinations of any six letters and numbers approved by the state.

ASSISTANT RESEARCHES LOTTERY

As a member of the Interstate Corporation Committee, I had been elected chairman of the Environmental Resources Committee of the Southern Legislative Conference. Virginia had entered into a compact with Maryland to see how we might clean up the Chesapeake Bay. I was in Annapolis meeting with Delegate Denny Minnick and Senator Bunk Athey discussing how we might raise the funds to accomplish this.

Delegate Minnick asked me, "Billy, why don't you introduce the lottery in Virginia?" I asked him, "What is a lottery?" He proceeded to explain what the lottery was all about and that the Maryland state income tax and the sales tax were the only two revenues that raised more money than it did. The lottery even raised more revenue than corporate income tax.

When the legislative session began in 1983, I had Legislative Services draft a lottery bill for me. However, I was not sure if I was going to introduce the bill. Knowing that there were strong feelings against gambling promoted by the state, I felt that this could damage my political future.

I had hired a legislative aide, Kathy Axon. She had finished law school at the University of Richmond but had not taken the law exam. She was the daughter of Peter Axon, who was the commonwealth attorney in Chesapeake. Still pondering over the drafted lottery bill, I asked, "Kathy will you go over to the State Library and do a little research on the lottery?"

About four hours later she came back with her hands filled with yellow legal pages. There was a gleam in her big blue eyes and her hands were trembling. I said, "Kathy, where in the hell have you been?"

She yelled at me, "O'Brien, put the damn bill in," and informed me, "we probably would not be here today if it had not been for the lottery. Lottery money was used to fund the Jamestown Expedition in 1607. They raised 1200 pounds in London with a lottery in 1606 to fund the expedition.

"Thomas Jefferson said, 'The lottery is a wonderful thing; it lays the taxation only upon the willing.' They funded the capital of Washington with a lottery and George Washington bought the first ticket. He didn't win a prize, but they did name the city after him."

I put the bill in the hopper and that began the toughest eight years of my life!

RVP010902-1/9/86-RICHMOND,VA.: Del J.W. "Billy" O'Brien (D-VA. Beach) grin
as he takes his seat 1/9 after announcing to the House that any delegate
wishing to sign his "Voluntary tax" bill should see him. The bill he was
referring to is his annual attempt to pass a lottery bill. UPI   jm/mojo

The Virginian-Pilot

Letters
Tuesday, May 17, 1983
Editorials

State Lottery for Education

Editor, *Virginian-Pilot*:

A distinguished educator, Dr. John Lope Franklin of Duke University, speaking at Norfolk State University's commencement exercises last weekend, reiterated what we have been hearing a lot about recently—the mediocrity of Virginia's public education system. Reasons cited are low and uniform salaries for our teachers, the need to improve the system of remunerating teachers and administrators, and improving the quality of our educational system.

Of course, any knowledgeable Virginian realizes this system of educational problems and teacher problems cannot be improved without money. In an editorial about Dr. Franklin's speech, The Pilot repeatedly asked the question, 'Now who pays?'', while speaking of the obvious answer—Virginia taxpayers by way of tax increases. Those of us who are already bearing the burden of high taxes do not want additional taxes to pay.

There is an alternative that is available and waiting which would provide the dollars sorely needed for our educational problems, create no new tax burdens and provide jobs for the disabled and elderly. Most of you have read of or heard about my idea for a state lottery. It certainly makes a lot of sense in that it is a voluntary tax, which can be put to use in eliminating Virginia's educational problems.

During this past session of the General Assembly, I introduced a bill providing for a state lottery referendum. If this bill had passed it would have given the voters the privilege of voting for a state lottery. I think that the voters of Virginia deserve the chance to choose between being taxed without their consent and a voluntary tax via a state lottery.

It is important to note that West Virginia, Maryland and Washington, D.C., have all passed lottery bills. North Carolina's lottery bill has passed the Senate and will soon go to the House of Representatives. If it passes the House, North Carolina will also have a lottery, leaving Virginia surrounded by states with lotteries. I wonder how much Virginia money will be going into neighboring state's lotteries?

Maryland's lottery is expected to net $200 million in 1983. Just think of what millions of dollars earned by a voluntary tax could do to improve Virginia's public education system?

J. W. (BILLY) O'BRIEN,
Delegate,
Eighty-Third District.
Virginia Beach.

THE CITIZENS THREATEN TO FIRE ME

Finally things were looking good for the lottery. The referendum had passed the Senate and the House. The citizens of the commonwealth were going to vote on the lottery. I was confident that we'd win, but it wasn't a sure thing. We needed all the favorable publicity that we could get. I was fielding a lot of calls from reporters to discuss the issues for the television news and doing as many interviews as I could. I had a pretty high profile.

One day Dr. Fred Bateman, superintendent of schools, called and said that he wanted to meet with me concerning my campaign for the passage of the referendum. As I walked to Dr. Bateman's office in the School Administration Building, I felt apprehensive and nervous.

"Billy, are you campaigning for this referendum on school time?" he asked.

"Well, I'm trying not to, but I'm getting a lot of phone calls from TV reporters," I replied.

His face became grim and stern. He said, "Do you realize that you're going to get us both fired if you take a favorable stand on this issue?"

Just what I needed. No job. What was he thinking? A favorable stand? I'd been vigorously campaigning for this for years.

The two powerful, but disgruntled citizens, had talked to Dr. Batsman and expressed the Bible-belt conviction that gambling was sinful and unChristian. They'd both said, in effect, "If Billy O'Brien campaigns for the lottery, he and you, Dr. Bateman, could lose your jobs."

I was prepared to go toe to toe with the Religious Right, but I never imagined that they would threaten to take away my livelihood if I didn't go along with their beliefs.

To placate Dr. Bateman, I said, "You can rest assured that I won't do anything on school time with this measure."

I left the office feeling furious and disgusted, thinking to myself, *All I ever wanted was to raise money for teachers. You'd think that the people in the City of Chesapeake would give me full support instead of threatening to fire me.*

That night I made a call to Ted Morrison, a good friend and fellow member of the House of Delegates. He was the smartest lawyer and best legislator I had ever met. I had served with him in the House for four years and couldn't stand him at first. I thought he was the biggest smart-ass I'd ever met.

That attitude changed during a golf trip with two other legislators and two lobbyists During this trip I roomed with Ted in a condo and we became close friends. Before we left, he said, "I've rented a house in the Fan Area of Richmond and I need someone to share the place during the next legislative session. Are you interested?" I said that I was. We became good friends and were sort of like the Odd Couple—a real smart-ass lawyer and a dumb-ass coach.

He was the best guy in the state for me to call about the problem with Dr. Bateman. I told him about the citizens who were trying to fire me.

He said, "Threatening a state legislator over a political position is a class-five felony. If you can prove that and press charges, they could go to the state penitentiary for five years."

Delegate Billy O'Brien and Delegate Ted Morrison. Staff photo by Bob Brown, *Richmond Times Dispatch*.

addresses the General Laws Committee during a public hearing on O'Brien's bill that calls for a statewide vote on a state lottery. The public hearing was held 1/20 but the committee did not vote on the measure. UPI jm/ Joe Mahoney

LOTTERY PAY SCANDAL

One of the worst things that ever happened in my life was during the campaign for the lottery. As you'll recall, I had a run-in with some influential individuals who had said that I shouldn't spend time campaigning for the lottery even on my own time. I considered prosecuting them, which would have meant, if convicted, they could be imprisoned for five years. After giving this matter much thought, I decided not to do so because they were unaware of the law and this would have been unfair to them.

As a way of resolving the conflict, I requested a leave of absence without pay so that I could devote my time campaigning for the lottery. There was so much public support for the lottery that a committee had been formed to support the effort. They had raised about twenty thousand dollars and the committee approached me with the idea of working for them full-time with pay. They agreed to pay me my salary as a teacher, which was $185 per day. Once we came to an agreement, one of the committee members released the news to the press that I would be working for them for pay.

When this news hit the press in Virginia Beach, every newspaper, every radio station, and every television station picked it up and ran a story saying that I was going to be paid by the lottery to get it passed. I got hundreds of calls from the press asking me why I was asking money from lottery companies. I couldn't tell them of the previous meeting with Dr. Bateman when we had been threatened of losing our jobs.

During a press conference about this situation, I felt totally humiliated. I was shaking as I stood at the podium in front of a packed room of journalists. I'd worked for eight years for the lottery trying to get it passed, and now I was afraid a scandal was going to get it defeated.

During the press conference I stated that I had spoken with the Virginia Attorney General, Mary Sue Terry, before making the decision to accept money for my campaigning efforts. She had told me that it would not be violating any state laws, nor would it be unethical to accept pay. However, that was going to be a difficult concept to get across to the people, especially with the press suggesting that it was unethical.

I told journalists from all over the state that I was quitting the lottery campaign and was going back to work in the Adult Education Center. I gave no speeches for the lottery nor did I give any interviews to TV or newspaper reporters until the lottery was approved by the voters.

We had a saying in the legislature that you should never foul up on a slow news day because every reporter who did not have anything to write about would write about how you fouled up. There is one thing you do as a football coach and a politician: never let the individual who has the pen and ink last get mad at you for not allowing him to do his job.

The lottery was a very hot topic in the state at that time, and I sincerely believed that when a newspaper reporter or a TV reporter had a slow news day, they would say to each other, "Let's go out to the Adult Education Center and interview Billy O'Brien and do a story about the lottery," and they did.

During my coaching career and my political career, I worked and achieved the reputation among all reporters as "Billy O'Brien is good ink." What that means is the coach will give you a very good story. That was the only error I made on school time at the Adult Education Center.

Del. O'Brien was criticized for trying to extract fees

from the lottery industry.

Chastened O'Brien Drops Role to Form Va. Lottery

By R.H. Melton
Washington Post Staff Writer

VIRGINIA BEACH, July 16—Del. J.W. (Billy) O'Brien Jr., Virginia's most visible advocate of state-sponsored gambling, announced today he will abandon that campaign after criticism of his attempt to extract sizable fees from lottery equipment vendors in exchange for his promotional efforts.

"I am doing this because my income and personal involvement have become the media focus" of the state's upcoming lottery referendum, O'Brien told reporters at a news conference here.

In a one-page statement, O'Brien, a Democratic member of the House of Delegates from this ocean resort city, said his decision was "in the best interest of the passage of the lottery." He then defended his recent request to be paid $185 per day by a group of lottery equipment makers and promptly left the hotel where the news conference was held, declining to answer questions.

O'Brien's emotional withdrawal from a lottery crusade he launched shortly after his election to the House in 1973 comes on the heels of a public relations disaster he caused this week when he said he needed the fees from lottery firms to make ends meet. He is on a leave of absence from his job as an adult education teacher in the city of Chesapeake, Va.

Lottery opponents promptly seized on O'Brien's remarks, saying they were an indication that lottery companies intended to "buy" their way into the state before the November referendum. At the same time, several equipment makers were left aghast by O'Brien's ill-timed request.

"We applaud . . . his stepping out of this controversy and putting the lottery ahead of his personal inter-

ests," said C. Gray Bethea Jr., the vice president and general counsel of Scientific Games Inc., the Atlanta-based lottery equipment giant that will contribute money to pro-lottery forces in Virginia.

Bethea said his firm, the world's largest supplier of "instant" lottery tickets, has learned that lottery referendums fail when campaigns promoting them lack "integrity."

"If a legislator who sponsors a bill in the Virginia legislature then turns around and as a private citizen solicits money to be the public proponent of that, there are problems with that approach," Bethea said. "Now that Billy—I should say Del. O'Brien—has recognized that, I applaud him."

Jeff Gregson, the executive director of a group of Virginia corporate executives opposed to a lottery, said O'Brien's decision "will not make any difference in the way we conduct our campaign."

If anything, some of Gregson's allies said they would have preferred that O'Brien continue to stump for the lottery. Although O'Brien was an enthusiastic campaigner for legalized gambling, many on both sides of the issue believed that the lanky former high school coach was not the lottery's most inspiring advocate.

Minutes before his news conference this morning, O'Brien was told—by his school employers, according to one associate—to rewrite his terse statement. The first version had O'Brien merely "stepping back" from the campaign and promising to help with the "coaching" of "a lottery team" so that "pro-lottery fans can be assured of a voice."

The prose was struck from the statement. Instead, O'Brien noted only that he remained committed to the lottery ideal.

"Unfortunately," he added, "the merits of the lottery itself were being ignored."

The Virginian-Pilot
AND
The Ledger-Star

RICHARD F. BARRY III, Publisher
CARL W. MANGUM, President
SANDRA M. ROWE, Executive Editor
JAMES C. RAPER, Managing Editor
WILLIAM H. WOOD, Editor

Published by
Landmark Communications, Inc.

FRANK BATTEN, Chairman
RICHARD F. BARRY III, President

POLITICS

O'Brien's lottery exit

He may be Virginia's "Mr. Lottery," but J.W. "Billy" O'Brien is also a member of the House of Delegates and hence doesn't belong on the pro-lottery interests' payroll in the campaign for voter approval of a state lottery in the Nov. 3 referendum.

So, the Virginia Beach lawmaker made the correct choice Thursday when he abandoned his plan to lead the pro-lottery forces for $185 a day.

A legal conflict of interest apparently did not exist here — Mr. O'Brien said Attorney General Mary Sue Terry issued an opinion stating that his paid role would violate no ethics laws. But the alliance was one the public understandably would be uncomfortable with.

For even though Mr. O'Brien is widely known as the General Assembly's most prominent and persistent advocate of a statewide lottery and his stated motive is to provide Virginia with a new source of revenue, it was clearly inappropriate for him to serve as a paid mouthpiece for those who will profit from the establishment of a lottery in Virginia: vendors who print lottery tickets and sell lottery equipment, to cite two examples. A public official, probably more than anyone else, needs to be guided in his actions by the appearance those actions create.

The pay question arose because Mr. O'Brien took an unpaid leave from his job as assistant director of the Chesapeake Adult Education Center to become full-time spokesman for the lottery. Now that he has stepped out of the referendum campaign, he will return to his school post.

The veteran lawmaker made his decision, he said, "because my income and personal involvement have become the media focus of the referendum. Unfortunately, the merits of the lottery itself were being ignored."

Mr. O'Brien's retreat is welcome. But his stated reason unfortunately leaves the impression that he still does not realize he shouldn't have placed himself in so questionable a position in the first place.

9/17 about his proposed lottery bill during a meeting of the House General Laws Committee at the State Capitol. O'Brien, who proposes a lottery bill virtually every session, offered his bill as a way to fund Virginia's future transportation needs. UPI jm/jm

THE LEDGER-STAR
Section C
Friday, January 14, 1983

Virginia Lottery Plan Is Again Resurrected

News item: Since the Washington, D.C. lottery began 6 months ago, 19,261,800 tickets have been sold.

When the football coach himself, Del. Billy O'Brien of Virginia Beach, called for a statewide lottery last year, his colleagues in the General Assembly blitzed hard, caught him behind the line of scrimmage and threw him for a loss.

O'Brien's bill to create a lottery in this commonwealth died in committee with a stake through its heart.

Well, here we go again. Twelve months after he was sacked on Capitol Square, O'Brien is again carrying a ball for a statewide lottery.

He calls it the workingman's dreamboat.

He says we need it now more than ever.

There is a new wrinkle in O'Brien's game plan.

If his fellow legislators threw his 1983 lottery bill for a loss on the grounds that a lottery is wicked, O'Brien is liable to introduce a bill calling for an end to all gaming in Virginia.

That includes bingo, friendly bets among golfers, the sweepstakes you participate in at the supermarket and in the places where they sell the Big Macs. Even contests like the one sponsored by this newspaper; the I-slam-dunked-Bob-the-sportswriter thing.

Let's end the double standard, he said. If a lottery is wicked, bingo is wicked.

"Let's do away with it all," the man said.

Or let's get smart and put in a statewide lottery.

The governor is talking about $305 million in budget deficits. He is hinting that the state treasury will be bare by midsummer. We could see another ice age before state employees get a raise.

According to O'Brien, we can reduce the hole in the state budget by $130–$150 million in the next two years if a statewide lottery becomes fact. His bill asks that the question of a lottery be decided by voters in a referendum come November.

"I see a lottery as a voluntary tax that most people would be happy to pay," O'Brien said earlier this week before pushing off to Richmond to find support for his bill.

O'Brien would set up a commission to decide how to conduct the lottery.

Some of our neighbors have it—Maryland, Pennsylvania, the District of Columbia. Eighteen states have put in a lottery. In Washington, D.C., they are calling it a huge success. Maybe bigger than the Redskins, even.

Since August, the city has seen $11.9 million deposited in the general fund thanks to the lottery. It costs $1 to play the daily lottery in Washington. You could be an instant winner—from $2 to $10,000. And if you are lucky enough to draw a $100 ticket, you become eligible for the grand prize of $1 million.

There have been two such winners in Washington, D.C. since summer. Two instant millionaires.

When they started the lottery up there, they printed 10 million tickets, figuring that they would last for 8 to 12 weeks. On the third day of the lottery, they were ordering more tickets. They've sold 19,261,800 lottery tickets as of last November.

Thirty percent of the money goes into the city's general fund to pave roads, put up streetlights and do other important things. Forty-eight percent of the income goes right back out in winnings. It's been such a success, this D.C. lottery, that the outfit picked to run it, the D.C. Lottery and Charitable Games Control Board, profited by $5,905,807.

Today, Washington; tomorrow, Virginia?

Maryland's state lottery brings in $175 million annually with 37 percent of that money going to higher education. Senior citizens in Pennsylvania share in the $152 million that lottery raises—old folks ride the buses for free in that state.

"The lottery will not rescue us from debt. Nor will it reduce taxes," O'Brien said. "But its revenue could forestall another tax increase."

He doubts if anyone will blow the rent money playing a lottery.

In a state which prides itself on tradition, O'Brien reminds us that a lottery is very much part of the past. When the Virginia Company's expedition to the new world was on the rocks, they held a lottery in England in 1612 and kept it afloat.

O'Brien's idea to raise more money for the state sounds like fun. What do you think?

Delegate William "Buster" O'Brien and Delegate Billy O'Brien. Staff photo by Bob Brown, *Richmond Times Dispatch*.

The Lottery O'Brien
By Shelley Rolfe
Richmond Times Dispatch
1/12/1985

Two O'Briens sit in the House of Delegates. Each is from Virginia Beach. Each has a William in the name. There is William R. O'Brien, who is known as Buster. And there is J. William O'Brien Jr., who is known as Billy.

Each occasionally is sent a General Assembly pay or expense check that is meant for the other. Citizens of Virginia Beach also have been known to confuse one O'Brien with the other.

Each has college football in his past. Buster O'Brien was a front-rank quarterback for the University of Richmond in the late 1960s. Billy O'Brien was a role player as an end at the University of North Carolina three decades ago. Buster O'Brien is a lawyer. Billy O'Brien is a school administrator, who was once a highly successful high school football coach.

Buster O'Brien is a Republican. He would like to be his party's 1985 nominee for attorney general. Billy O'Brien is a Democrat. He does not aspire to higher office. He, however, is not without ambition. If he had his way, citizens of Virginia, who now invest in such things as the Maryland and District of Columbia lotteries, would do their spending at home.

Billy O'Brien is the lottery O'Brien, the man who would establish a state lottery to fatten Virginia's treasury. He pursues his goal with single-minded purpose. He has done this ever since he was told by a Maryland legislator that, next to the income tax, the lottery was that state's largest revenue source. With a reedy voice, O'Brien invokes visions of sugarplums. He invariably carries documents that deal with the uplifting effect of lotteries, past and present

"In 1611 in Virginia...," he says. Well, in 1611, reports one of the papers he carries, a lottery helped underwrite the cost of colonization. O'Brien also likes to call a lottery the "workingman's rainbow."

On the day the 1985 Assembly session opened, O'Brien, as he had done the previous two years, introduced lottery legislation that calls for a statewide referendum before one could go into operation.

The next day, O'Brien, after surveying the snowy, gray scene from his legislative office window, began recalling the fate of his first two lottery measures. Two years ago: killed on the House floor. The two O'Briens stood together on the question. Last year it was killed in committee.

Despite the record, O'Brien remains sanguine. In Virginia, some things cannot be rushed. He is not daunted.

Somehow the opposition of religious leaders and the fears that a lottery might somehow lead to incursions by organized crime will be overcome. Somehow his fellow legislators will begin thinking of the state's take from a lottery, money that could be used for education and the elderly. This year he has added money for the cleanup of Chesapeake Bay to his something-for-everybody grab bag.

O'Brien believes 1985 prospects have been enhanced by West Virginia's decision to set up a lottery later this year. "In West Virginia they realized organized crime was not going to come in with a lottery," he said, hoping he was making points.

In the past O'Brien has tried to make other points by regaling listeners with tales of the brisk business Maryland country stores near the Virginia border have done selling lottery tickets to Virginians. Now his country store repertoire has been expanded to include near-the-border West Virginia stores that he reports are preparing for an onslaught of Virginians.

O'Brien announced he also had been heartened by the fact that Gov. Chuck Robb, in his State of the Commonwealth speech, did not say he would veto lottery legislation. But on the other hand, O'Brien was told, Robb didn't say he'd sign it either. O'Brien resumed his study of the landscape.

O'Brien has become a player as well as a believer. Not too long ago, he sent the lottery authorities in Maryland a $52 check. Each week he is mailed a one-dollar ticket; with a dramatic flourish, he produced this week's mail from Annapolis.

There has yet to be a newspaper or TV story on sudden wealth raining down on him. His total winnings: zero. Again he is sanguine and undaunted.

"I realize I have as much chance of winning as I have of being struck by lightning," O'Brien said. "But this is the only chance I have of becoming a millionaire."

Delegate Seeking State Lottery
Comes Up With Right Numbers
By Tyler Whitley

Richmond Times Dispatch, 08-15-1985

VIRGINIA BEACH (UPI)—Del. J.W. "Billy" O'Brien can use himself in a testimonial the next time he tries to push a lottery for Virginia.

He cashed in on the Maryland numbers game this week for $984.

"It's amazing," he said as he held a check from the Maryland treasury. "I've always said that I'd like to win the thing, but I knew my chances were one in a million.

"I guess I'm doing better with the lottery up in Maryland than I am in Virginia," he said.

O'Brien has tried unsuccessfully since 1982 to persuade the Virginia General Assembly that a lottery would be beneficial for the state and bring in more than $250 million during an era in which budgets are strapped.

"Boy, you talk about irony," O'Brien said of his winnings.

The legislation O'Brien has pushed would set up a statewide referendum for voters to decide whether there should be legalized numbers.

In his research last year, O'Brien discovered a subscription application to the Maryland lottery.

"I figured, 'what the heck,' and sent it in with $100," he said.

O'Brien said he could not remember which numbers he chose, but suspected they were variations of those worn by some of his best football players when he was coach at Great Bridge High School.

The U.S. Postal Service in June ordered states with lotteries to stop selling tickets by mail to nonresidents.

The lawmaker is unopposed in November's election, and plans to push for the lottery again next year. But he said members of the chamber should not expect to see him waving his ticket on the floor of the House as a prop.

O'Brien Gets New Chance on Lottery Bill
By Bill Byrd
The Virginian Pilot, September 5, 1986

RICHMOND—Del. J. W. "Billy" O'Brien, Jr. will get another chance later this month to ask the General Assembly to pass the perennial lottery bill.

The Virginia Beach Democrat said Thursday that House Speaker A. L. Philpott who ruled the lottery legislation can be conferred during the special Assembly session beginning Sept. 15. The session will deal with transportation issues, including Gov. Gerald Baliles' multibillion-dollar road-building program.

Philpott decided that the lottery proposal is relevant to the purpose of the special session, because O'Brien has said some proceeds from the games would be used for transportation projects.

The speaker "said to me, 'If you have a lottery addressed to transportation, then it appears to me to be germane. I wish you wouldn't do it, but you can introduce it,'" O'Brien said in an interview Thursday. With the procedural obstacle cleared, O'Brien said, he will file the bill with the clerk of the House today.

The measure would allow the voters to decide in a Feb. 3 referendum whether they want a state-run lottery, with the proceeds to be used for transportation projects.

O'Brien said he believes the lottery could raise more than $350 million a year for roads and other projects "once we get rolling."

He said Maryland, which has about 1 million fewer people than Virginia, is able to collect that amount annually through its state-run games.

Last year, the State Finance Committee estimated that a state lottery could bring Virginia up to $104 million a year; other state estimates have put the annual revenue at close to $180 million.

O'Brien's lottery bills have met defeat either in committee or on the House floor, five times, but Thursday he said he thought the measure's chances were good.

"I sure do think I've got a better show," he said. Many legislators are searching for ways to avoid raising taxes and might settle on the lottery as the best way to come up with the road money, he said.

"I can get it passed on the House floor," O'Brien predicted. Only once, in 1983, has his lottery proposal made it that far. Every other year it has been killed by the House General Laws Committee.

The Virginia Beach delegate said he expects that the bill this time will be referred to the House Finance Committee.

He said he has not gauged support for the bill among the panel's members.

He is heartened, however, by the "great reaction" among the public to his proposal. He said many Virginians would prefer the lottery to increases in the sales, gasoline and titling taxes. Baliles wants all three raised to pay for roads.

O'Brien also said he is prepared to offer an amendment that responds to criticism that the lottery victimizes the poor. The amendment would make anyone receiving welfare ineligible to win lottery prizes.

Dialogue
O'Brien Defends State Lottery

From Del. J.W. (Billy) O'Brien 83rd District House of Delegates

In response to the article concerning the State lottery, I would like to present the following observations:

Organized crime does not infiltrate a state-run lottery. In fact, it does away with many illegally run numbers games prominent in many urban cities. We have no organized crime in the ABC Commission.

A voluntary tax does not transgress on the poor. Statistics indicate that 85 percent of the people who participate in a lottery make between $18,000 and $56,000 per year.

If Virginia had two pari-mutuel racetracks, they would only generate approximately $2 million per year in revenue, and it would take this $2 million to sophisticate our state police to monitor this situation. Also, organized crime does enter into pari-mutuel betting. I am also opposed to casino betting.

The lottery in Maryland generated approximately $200 million per year and it is estimated that about 25 percent of this money comes out of Northern Virginia.

The Municipal League has advocated a one-cent increase in the sales tax, and I need not remind you that this tax applies to food. I think this is unconscionable. A lottery would be an alternative to this tax.

I noted that the Silver-Haired Legislature, hardly a radical group, went on record in favor of a lottery this past year.

There is one certain way to resolve this question—schedule a referendum on the subject this fall and let the voice of the people decide the issue. Surely no legislator or citizen can object to letting the citizens of this Commonwealth be the final arbiters of this matter.

In a state which prides itself on tradition, O'Brien reminds us that a lottery is very much part of the past. When the Virginia Company's expedition to the new world was on the rocks, they held a lottery in England in 1612 and kept it afloat.

O'Brien's idea to raise more money for the state sounds like fun. What do you think?

House Speaker Tom Moss and Delegate "Buster" O'Brien. Staff photo by
Bob Brown, *Richmond Times Dispatch*.

Virginia's Lottery Could Hit Jackpot
in Dollars from N.C.
Associated Press

RALEIGH—North Carolina lawmakers say they're worried that a lottery referendum approved by the Virginia General Assembly may take millions of dollars from the Tar Heel state as residents head north to play the game.

"North Carolina is not Virginia, but I think it will give more fuel to lottery proponents," Rep. Coy Privette, R-Cabarrus, said of Virginia's referendum.

"My immediate comment is, 'Let's see what Virginia does about it,'" he added.

On Saturday, just before it was to adjourn for the year, Virginia's legislature approved bills to establish a lottery board and a referendum in November on a state lottery.

The next move in Raleigh seems to belong to Rep. Frank E. Rhodes, R-Forsyth, who introduced a bill for a lottery referendum that narrowly passed the House in 1985. Rhodes said he plans to introduce a similar bill within two weeks.

Lottery proponents may try to maneuver sponsorship of the referendum into Democratic hands to increase its chance of passage. But Rhodes said he feels no pressure to turn the bill over to a member of the House majority.

Sen. Kenneth Royall Jr., D-Durham, said Virginia was feeling the effect of lotteries in neighboring Maryland and Washington, D.C. Royall said North Carolina would feel the same effect if Virginia has a lottery.

Royall sponsored a lottery-referendum bill in the 1985 Senate that died in a 24–24 vote when Lt. Gov. Robert B. Jordan III declined to break the tie. Royall said that he does not have a lottery bill under way but that he will not wait to see what Virginia does before he takes action.

Already, Rhodes said, North Carolinians are spending an incalculable amount of money to buy lottery tickets through truck drivers and out-of-state relatives. If Virginia enacts a lottery, he said, millions of North Carolina dollars will benefit Virginia.

He said his bill, if approved by the legislature and the voting public, would use a lottery to generate about $200 million a year for an education fund.

The bill would also forbid the legislature to reduce its

normal appropriations for education, so the $200 million would be a real increase, Rhodes said.

"I agree with the fact that throwing money at education is not going to cure its ills," Rhodes said. "But properly directed, it can work wonders. And it can also help to attract better, quality teachers and to stop the exodus of our better quality teachers to private industry—or halt it by paying them a professional salary."

Privette said the message of a state-sponsored lottery is contrary to the values the state tries to instill in public schools.

The experience in other states has proven lotteries to be no help to education budgets, either, he said. Legislators compensate for the windfall from the lottery by reducing other spending for education, he said.

Still, teachers are among the major forces pushing for a lottery in this state, Privette said, citing statements by the North Carolina Association of Educators.

Delegate Billy O'Brien. Staff photo by Bob Brown, *Richmond Times Dispatch*.

Delegate Billy O'Brien. Staff photo by Bob Brown, *Richmond Times Dispatch*.

Three of Four Former Governors Line Up Against Lottery
By Tyler Whitley, *Richmond Times Dispatch* Staff Writer

Three of Virginia's four living former governors oppose a state-sponsored lottery.

The fourth, former Gov. Albertis S. Harrison Jr., declined to comment on the issue, because, as a retired Virginia Supreme Court justice, he sometimes hears cases before that court. Harrison, governor from 1962 to 1966, said the lottery still could develop into a legal issue.

Former Governors Linwood Holton, Mills E. Godwin Jr. and Charles S. Robb oppose the lottery.

Holton and Godwin said they have lent their names to organizations planning to fight the proposal when it is submitted to Virginia voters in a referendum this fall.

"I just cannot bring myself to accept that form of financing Virginia's government, which is based on the purest form of gambling," said Holton, the first Republican governor elected in Virginia this century. Holton was governor from 1970 to 1974.

"A lottery sucks money out of the economic groups that can least afford it," Holton said. "It creates an addiction that you can get something for nothing. That's false; you can't."

Holton, who lives in McLean and practices law in Washington, said a lottery takes money away from lower-income persons to pay for projects that "more affluent people ought to be paying for."

He said he has authorized his name to be used on the letterhead of a group opposed to the lottery, but he expected that other commitments would prevent him from taking an active role in an anti-lottery campaign.

Reached yesterday at his home in Suffolk, Godwin said, "I never supported a lottery in the past and don't intend to now. I don't think Virginia needs this innovation in its revenue."

A lottery "bodes more ill than it does good for the people of Virginia in the long run," said Godwin.

He said he had no plans to campaign against a lottery, but he has allied himself with "Free Enterprise Against a Lottery," a group of prominent businessmen opposing the state-sponsored gambling enterprise.

Godwin was governor from 1966 to 1970 and from

1974 to 1978, the first time as a Democrat, the second time as a Republican.

Robb, governor from 1982 to 1986, told the General Assembly in 1985 that he opposed a lottery. In a recent interview with *The Richmond News Leader*, he said he considers advertising that Maryland and other states use to promote a lottery "unseemly."

"If Virginia moves toward a lottery, I would hope they wouldn't move in the direction of state promotion of a lottery," he said.

The General Assembly adopted legislation last week restricting the type of advertising that a lottery board could use. Only informational advertising would be allowed. So-called "inducement" advertising would be prohibited.

Gov. Gerald L. Baliles, who succeeded Robb, endorsed a lottery referendum in his opening address to the 1987 General Assembly in January. He added, however, that he had reservations about a lottery as a way of raising money. He expressed those same reservations during his campaign for governor in 1985.

He has declined to say whether he will campaign for or against a lottery during this fall's referendum campaign.

The legislation agreed to by the Assembly would submit the issue to the people in a Nov. 3 election. If voters approve, a department would be set up to administer the lottery, which state officials estimate could net the state $100 million in its first full year of operation.

Public opinion polls indicate that a majority of Virginians favor the lottery.

The opposition of the former governors, however, is expected to give a boost to opponents, who already have begun organizing against the issue. Former Attorney General J. Marshall Coleman announced Thursday he would campaign actively against a lottery.

The proponents, meanwhile, have not set up an organization. Del. J.W. "Billy" O'Brien. Jr. D-Virginia Beach, the chief lottery proponent in the General Assembly, said he expected suppliers of lottery equipment to pay for a pro-lottery campaign.

Conflict Issue Grips Assembly in Deadline Push
By BILL BYRO and WARREN FISKE
Staff writers
Virginian Pilot

RICHMOND—The General Assembly on Saturday virtually assured that Virginians will go to the polls in November to decide if they want a state-run lottery.

All that is needed is the approval of Gov. Gerald L. Baliles, who has said he would sign a lottery bill if the lawmakers put one on his desk.

As Virginia's legislators struggled toward a late-night adjournment, they were deadlocked on one final, major issue: changes in the conflict-of-interest law that governs their ethics.

Hours before their scheduled adjournment, both the House of Delegates and the Senate passed compromise legislation setting up a state lottery if the voters approve the idea in a Nov. 3 referendum. The bill cleared the House on a 61–39 vote and squeaked through the Senate, 21–18. The bill now goes to the governor.

"I'm elated...I have the same feeling you have when you go into the locker room after a big game," said the House's principal lottery backer, Del. J.W. "Billy" O'Brien Jr., a former high school football coach.

Backers of the measure in both houses said Saturday that the voters deserve a chance to decide the issue.

"The people tell me that they want the right to vote," said House Majority Leader Thomas W. Moss Jr., D-Norfolk, in an impassioned floor speech. "What are we afraid of? That the people of the commonwealth just might want a lottery?"

Saturday's action came just hours after the lottery seemed headed for death in the 1987 session. The House on Friday stunned backers of legalized gambling by trouncing a compromise bill that bore no restrictions on advertising the lottery.

In a meeting that at times was acrimonious, a committee appointed to try to hammer out a final compromise agreed to a bill that would sharply limit lottery advertising, restrict the powers of the proposed lottery agency's directors and increase the authority of its five-member board.

The compromise worked, and the House reversed course. "If it hadn't," O'Brien said, "there would have been some embarrassed people."

Anti-lottery Groups Expect to be Outspent
By Bill Byrd, Staff Writer, May 16, 1987
Virginia News

RICHMOND—Anti-gambling forces now say that they probably will be outspent by pro-lottery groups in this fall's referendum campaign but that they expect to raise enough money to put their message on television.

Anti-lottery groups expect to raise about $750,000, said Jeff Gregson, executive director of Free Enterprisers Against Lottery, a group made up of conservative business and political leaders. FEAL expects to collect about $500,000, enough to mount a three-week television campaign in October, Gregson said Friday. The voters will decide on Nov. 3 whether the state should have a lottery.

The president of a second anti-lottery group, this one composed primarily of church and civic bodies, said his group probably will raise only about $275,000.

"That's an ambitious goal for us," said former Alexandria Del. Richard Hobson, president of Virginians Against State-Sponsored Gambling. He said his group plans a "grass-roots" effort against the lottery and also will use mass mailings to voters to raise money and spread the anti-lottery message.

Gregson predicted last month that lottery opponents could raise a total of $1 million, but on Friday he termed that estimate "an outside figure...With three-quarters of a million dollars, I think we can do what we want to do with that."

Gregson said he was "absolutely" sure pro-lottery forces would outspend the two anti-gambling organizations. "I think that between $1 million and $1.5 million in spending by pro-lottery organizations is very probable," he said. "I have a feeling the bulk will come from the games companies. They'll be pouring money into the pro-lottery campaign."

Lottery operating companies, such as Scientific Games Inc. of Atlanta, have heavily bankrolled campaigns to set up state-sponsored gambling in other states, such as Florida and California.

Gregson questioned whether a Virginia Beach telemarketing company hired by pro-lottery forces would be able to meet its goal of raising $1.5 million. Jan McCrary, director of telecommunications for CTP Marketing and

127

Communications, said on Thursday that her company plans to contact 700,000 homes and businesses by telephone.

McCrary said each household will be asked to contribute $20 to the lottery campaign; small businesses will be requested to make $100 contributions and larger corporations will be asked to donate $1,000.

McCrary's company was hired by Virginians for a State Lottery, a group headed by Del. J. W. "Billy" O'Brien, D-Virginia Beach. O'Brien this year successfully sponsored legislation setting up the November referendum.

"I know what it costs to make 700,000 telephone calls. The cost of getting something done like that ain't cheap," Gregson said Friday. "It's an expensive operation to implement. If they can do something like that, more power to them, but I have real reservations about that."

Hobson said Virginians Against State-Sponsored Gambling currently has only $6,000 in its treasury. The group expects to raise much of its money through church organizations, such as the Virginia Conference of the United Methodist Church and various Baptist bodies, Hobson said. So far, however, church support has been "haphazard," he added.

Virginians Against State-Sponsored Gambling will emphasize "grass-roots, get-out-the-vote" efforts, Hobson said. Local committees will be formed in cities and counties; a local chapter already has formed in Lynchburg, he said.

The group also will use mail appeals to voters, both to persuade them to vote against the lottery and to encourage them to donate money. The anti-gambling group has not yet signed a contract with a direct-mail firm, Hobson said.

The former Alexandria delegate also said his group will sponsor debates and forums on the lottery and will buy a limited amount of newspaper advertising.

"We do expect an uphill fight," Hobson said. But forces fighting parimutuel betting in 1978 raised less than $150,000 and still managed to defeat the issue, he noted. Hobson, a legislator at the time, played a leading role in the anti-parimutuel effort.

O'Brien this week said a recent poll of Virginians continues to show strong support for the lottery. Sixty-two percent of those contacted in an April poll said they would vote for it, he said.

The poll was conducted by Hickman-Maslin Co. of Washington, a political consulting firm which often provides services to Democratic candidates. Scientific Games "paid for part of it," O'Brien said.

Officials at Scientific Games' headquarters in suburban Atlanta referred calls this week to Maria Garcia, a Denver consultant. Repeated telephone calls to her went unreturned.

NO: It Could Undermine Society's Very Foundation
By Mills E. Godwin Jr.

In VIRGINIA'S Declaration of Rights, George Mason, in 1776, wrote "that no free government nor the blessings of liberty can be preserved to any people, but by a firm adherence to justice, moderation, temperance, frugality and virtue..." In this bicentennial year of our nation's Constitution, we are reminded over and over again of these words.

Are we to permit the Virginia celebration to be turned into a travesty on Nov. 3 by ignoring these basic principles and encouraging a scheme that carries the potential of undermining the very foundation of our society?

This is more than a rhetorical question. The proposed state lottery embodies a very real threat through an attempt to pervert the government of our commonwealth into a promoter of gambling, by the force of law, and encouraging resort to its devices to the enrichment of the few and the enslavement of the unwary by enticing promises of "something for nothing."

The wily professional gambling promoters, whose only interest is broadening the base of their clientele, attempt to paint their mission as one of philanthropic goals—huge benefits to the state treasury, avoidance of a tax increase and a wholesome "recreation" for the citizenry.

My study of the facts convinces me to the contrary beyond all doubt. In addition to putting the government into the business of operating the lottery—a field totally foreign to the proper functions of government—such an alliance would reverse the whole image and purposes of public administration in Virginia. Government without constant consideration of moral issues and the true welfare of the people is a mockery and an abdication of its basic responsibilities.

It is no accident that Virginia enjoys the reputation of operating one of the best systems of government in the United States, with the welfare and interests of the taxpayers foremost on its agenda. And it is not just by chance that the attorney general and former attorneys general have taken their public stand against the lottery, along with a large number of the members of our General Assembly. They have done so on the basis of their own knowledge and study of the subject. As officials responsible for making and enforcing the laws, and ensuring fair treatment for all, they recognize that lotteries tend to create a climate altogether antagonistic to the principles which most Virginians have accepted as basic for the past two centuries.

Our free-enterprise system provides the foundation for our prosperity and the quality of life we enjoy. The preservation and continued success of this system certainly would be endangered by the renunciation of these truths by recurrence to a lottery. The lotteries preach and teach the exact opposite to free enterprise, emphasizing the something-for-nothing approach and capitalizing on the weakness of human nature, at times, to yield to exaggerated blandishments picturing tantalizing prospects of possible financial windfalls. Unfortunately, in the process of gilding that glistening pot of gold at the end of the mythical rainbow, many of our impressionable citizens—young and old—will become habitual investors and certain losers at the expense of their education, their livelihoods and their sense of initiative, creativity and responsibility as members of the body politic.

Furthermore, when we analyze the obligations of government, we find no constitutional, legislative, or universal mandate to take the lottery route to meeting, or supplementing, the normal and proper avenues for rating the funds required to carry out the functions of state government. It is much more equitable to operate under a fair and logical system calling for levies in proportion to ability to pay, rather than to turn to a program which is sure to become a heavy burden on the many who can ill afford to be the source of funds which go to the opulent promoters and the very few "winners" when the drawings are announced.

The fact that other states have state-sponsored lotteries should carry no persuasion in Virginia. The other states have had varying experience, certainly not altogether good; and I am not apprised of any state in which a lottery has resulted in relief to the taxpayers by reduction in levies or avoidance of additional taxes.

Mention has been made by some of the lottery advocates that lotteries were employed in colonial times, but they do not point out that they were short lived and were actually thrown out during the first half of the 19th century as the most dangerous and prolific inventions in our history.

THE FORTUNATE present state of fiscal affairs in Virginia, reflecting a treasury surplus of more than $150 million, certainly should be proof sufficient that the need for lottery revenues is non-existent. No amount of money siphoned out of the economy—with no productive attributes whatever—is worth the risk of ruining our whole system of sound and rational administration.

The "take" by equitable taxation definitely is to be preferred over a gambling venture, which, it is estimated, may absorb nearly two-thirds of every dollar of revenue before the state treasury receives one cent.

Finally, it is important that the voters of Virginia become aware of the fact that a lottery law already is on the statute books, and unless we say "NO" at the polls on Nov. 3 there will be a lottery in being on Dec 1, 1987.

I am not convinced that the broad spectrum of voters in Virginia are so disinterested or uninformed as to permit a distressing event, such as the introduction of a lottery, to occur in this commonwealth.

I urge every voter to carefully weigh this issue now confronting us and to mark his ballot against when he goes to the polling booth.

(Mills E. Godwin Jr., a former governor of Virginia, is a member of the Honorary Advisory Committee of Free Enterprisers Against Lottery.)

CIVIC LEAGUE MEETING IN PORTSMOUTH, VIRGINIA
1987
Port Norfolk

Del. Billy O'Brien: Good evening, ladies and gentlemen. I feel somewhat like I'm almost home. I was raised over in Parkview, my family coming here in 1936. My daddy was a machinist in the Navy Yard and I've fond memories of playing ball with Potsey Clise and Mata White. Nice to see Aunt Louise back there, I think some place. Let me point out again, I want to say just a little bit about how I got into politics. I worked in a hardware store in Portsmouth when I was very young. A man came in there one day, he said, "Boy, I want to buy half a stove pipe." And this is the biggest, ugliest, meanest man I have ever seen in my life. And I said, "Sir, we can't sell you half a stove pipe. We can sell you a whole stove pipe." He said, "Boy, you go back there and you tell your boss that I want to buy half a stove pipe." So, I did. And I went back and I said, "Boss, there is the biggest, ugliest, meanest man I've ever seen wants to buy half a stove pipe." And I looked behind me and he was right behind me. And I said, "And this fine gentleman wants to buy the other half." I'm gonna tell you one little story. I've been a teacher now for 34 years. I'll tell you a little teacher story. It seems this teacher had a class to identify famous sayings. So she asked the class who said "Give me liberty, or give me death." And no one in the class knew. There was this little Japanese girl who had only been over here 18 months got up. And she said, "St. John's Church, 1775, Richmond, Virginia, Patrick Henry." And the teacher said, "Oh, that's so nice. I'm so proud of you. But I'm a little concerned that none of you knew this answer." So she said, "Who said this. I shall return." No one in the class knew anything. Finally this little Japanese girl who had only been over here for 18 months got up and said, "1942, the Philippines, General Douglas MacArthur." And the teacher said, "That's correct. But I'm just ashamed of this class. Here she has only been over here 18 months, and knew all these statements." And at the back of the room somebody said, "To heck with the Japanese." The little girl got up and said, "Detroit, Michigan, 1984, Chrysler Motors."

I bet you thought I was going to talk about the lottery. I'm going to talk a little bit about the Pharmaceutical Assistance Contract for the Elderly. Now this legislation is in place in 13 states now. And do you know what that does? It says that anyone who is over 65 years of age who cannot qualify for Medicaid and who makes less than $15,000 a year, can apply to the Department of Aging, and get a card for $4.00 a month. And then with this $4.00 a month card they can have every prescription they need. And that would cost the Commonwealth of Virginia $75 million. And I don't think that's a bad way to spend the proceeds of a lottery. They do it now in 13 different states and I'm sure you are well aware that when people get a little age on them they have to go to the pharmacy for prescriptions they need. I've got that legislation in place right now. Didn't pass last year. But upon the approval of the citizens of the Commonwealth of the lottery, that bill will become law. I don't think that's too bad. You say, "Well, we don't need these funds in Virginia." Let me tell you something, ladies and gentlemen. The Federal Government is paying $183 billion a year just on interest payments alone on the Federal debt. And we have money coming down the Federal Government for Impact Aid for your schools, for your mental health, for your handicapped, and it's deficit spending, so we're going to need these funds. They built roads and schools and canals in colonial times. Thomas Jefferson said lottery was a wonderful thing. It lays the taxation only upon the willing. When we built the Nation's Capitol, we didn't have enough money. So they started a lottery. And George Washington bought the first ticket. He didn't win the lottery but they named the city after him. So, you know, in this year of our Constitution, I don't think it would be too bad of an idea to go back doing the things our founding fathers accomplished. Okay, now the next thing you'll say is a disproportionate number of poor people will put faith in the lottery. Well, that's a myth. It's untrue. Eighty-five percent of the people who participate in the lottery make between $18,000 and $56,000 a year. So it doesn't transgress on the poor. And, you know, it bothers me a little bit that people would try to dictate to the poor how to spend their discretionary money. Kind of indicating that just because you're poor, you're dumb. I don't think that's fair. Not to allow the people of this Commonwealth to vote on this proposition is a view that is guilty of elitist paternalism. I don't think that that type of intellect is worthy of a state that produced people such as Madison, Jefferson, and Monroe who believed that ordinary people could express good judgement and common sense if given the opportunity to do so. Okay, the next thing the people are going to say is that organized crime is going to get into this measure. The Mafia is going to come down here and that's not true. In the Richmond area alone there's a $50 million illegal numbers game going on right now. Grand jury investigation said so. So we already have a lottery in Virginia. Just a matter of who is going to profit, the crooks or the state. In Northern Virginia, the illegal numbers game is almost non-existent due to the proximity of the Maryland and DC lottery. And with the computers that we now have, it's virtually impossible to have fraud in the lottery. That's the only prize which you're going to get if you try to cheat with the lottery is a pair of handcuffs. Now, let me say one other thing. This happened the other day. The Fraternal Order of Police has endorsed the lottery. Now, as far as your casino and pari-mutuel, I'm opposed to both. I'm opposed to that because that will bring the problems, but the lottery, that's not the case. Let me just tell you one other thing about pari-mutuel. If we had two tracks in this Commonwealth it would only bring in $2 million in revenue. And it would take that $2 million in revenue to pay our police force to monitor it. So I'm opposed to both those entities. Now, they will say it will increase compulsive gambling. That's not true either. It takes horse racing, it takes the immediate action, the euphoria you get when a horse crosses the finish line. That's not true in the lottery. We get to wait six days. It's not the same thing in playing the stock market where you call your broker and put what you want and the next day you read it in the paper on the futures and commodities. That type of thing does create compulsive gambling, but not the lottery, because it's too slow. You'll say that state lotteries don't produce much money and are expensive to administer. That's not true either. Let me give you a breakdown of the dollar in Maryland. A dollar ticket in Maryland, 47 cents of the dollar goes to the lottery winners, 45 cents of the dollar goes to the state, 5 cents of the dollar goes to the store who sells it and it takes 3 cents of that dollar to administer it. Now I've got documented evidence over there on that. Now, when we're talking about revenue, Maryland makes $327 million a year on lottery sales. The Commonwealth of Virginia has a million more people than they've got. Let me tell you where the largest retail outlet of Maryland lottery tickets is. It's in Colonial Beach, Virginia, a little store sold $2 million worth of lottery tickets. The only way you can get there from Maryland is by boat. You can drive up out on a pier in Colonial Beach, Virginia, and buy Maryland lottery tickets. I don't think those people in Maryland are coming across by boat and buying lottery tickets. I think Virginians are subsidizing Maryland's schools and roads and police to the tune of 30% of their take. Now, I estimate the net will be $400–450 million a year in revenue in Virginia. That's about the same amount that would equate out to 1% increase in sales tax. And just think about this, ladies and gentlemen, we've got 450 miles of border down between North Carolina and Virginia. And I'm sure they'd like to do the same thing that we've been doing to Maryland for a long time. I'm sure they'd like to subsidize our schools and roads. And let me tell you something, ladies and gentlemen, when you purchase a lottery ticket, there are no losing tickets. There are no losing tickets. Someone either wins the prize or some need of the state is a winner such as mental health, education, the elderly, the pharmaceutical assistance contract for the elderly. So there are no losing tickets. Now you say, well, will it reduce taxes? No, it won't reduce taxes. But I'll tell you what it will do, it'll forestall another increase in the sales tax that was passed in the last mini-session to fund road construction. And I'm sure you're quite well aware that that applies to food. Ladies and gentlemen, we raise taxes in inappropriate ways. We encourage people to drink whiskey and to smoke cigarettes so we can tax that. And I guess worse of all, we have a tax on food. So this is an inappropriate way of raising taxes as of now. I'm going to conclude by saying the lottery is a form of gambling with three exceptions: it's inexpensive to administer, a little investment by the individual, and it's easy to insulate from the inevitable pressures of organized crime and politics. And last, but not least, it's a voluntary situation.

When He Rises, It's a Bet Lottery Will Be the Topic

Del. J.W. "Billy" O'Brien Jr. merely has to rise from his chair in the House of Delegates chamber to open the topic of a state lottery. He doesn't have to say the word.

O'Brien, a Virginia Beach Democrat who has introduced lottery bills year after year, did just that yesterday as he announced he would welcome co-patrons on a "voluntary tax measure."

The bill is the second now before the Assembly, since a slightly different lottery bill was profiled by state Sen. Clive L. DuVal II, D-Fairfax County.

Both measures call for a referendum to put the lottery question directly to voters, but they differ in how money raised by the lottery and not paid out to winners or spent to operate the game would be allocated.

DuVal's bill would split proceeds between education and programs for the elderly. O'Brien's would send the money to the state general fund.

The latter proposition seems designed to please the powerful Sen. Edward E. Willey, D-Richmond, who has opposed lottery bills in the past but has indicated this year he may be softening.

Willey is chairman of the Senate Finance Committee, one of two panels that largely determine how the general fund is budgeted.

Preliminary results of a Virginia Commonwealth University poll released this week show a majority of Virginians favor creation of a state lottery.

A Gallery of Great Virginians

George Washington

Thomas Jefferson

J W 'Billy' O'Brien

Commentary: Lottery Makes More Sense Than Ever
By Robert Wimer, Editorial Page Editor
Richmond Times Dispatch
09/07/1986

With an array of proposals lying in wait to raise taxes so the state can embark on a new road program, Del. J.W. "Billy" O'Brien Jr. is getting another attack of lottery fever. I feel a touch of it spreading out this way.

State-run lotteries are fun and exciting. I'm ready to plunk down a buck at the corner market on a chance to win two or five or even a hundred. O'Brien, a Virginia Beach Democrat, has wanted it for years. He's going to give it another try at the special session of the General Assembly on Sept. 15.

Is the assembly, which has snuffed out at least four previous proposals for a lottery, ready? Even in face of the need to raise an additional $6.3 billion in revenues over the next decade to pay for roads the governor says are needed to transport the state into the next century?

Committees in the House of Delegates have made short shrift of several earlier O'Brien proposals. This time around, they should give the revenue-raising measure more serious consideration.

At the very least, despite some individual reservations, the assembly members ought to let the state's voters decide for themselves whether Virginia is ready for a state lottery. Heretofore the legislature has balked at even submitting the question to the people in the form of a referendum. A majority seems to be telling the people they don't want to take this democracy of ours too far.

As a practical matter, a lottery would generate much-needed revenues for the state. A Senate Finance Committee report estimated late last year that a lottery could earn up to $105 million annually for the state. If that money were earmarked for roads, it would more than displace 3 cents of the proposed 4-cent increase in the state gasoline tax. Or it would nearly cover the proposed 2 percent boost in the vehicle titling tax.

Assuming a modest 10 percent growth per year, which those who track the lottery industry say is possible, the lottery earnings could generic at a minimum nearly $1.2 billion during the 10-year road construction program.

What are the myths that lottery opponents have spread across the years to keep the proposal under wraps? The principal criticisms, as I understand them, are these:

- Gambling is immoral.
- The state ought not sanction gambling.
- A lottery will increase violent crime.

- A lottery will hurt those most who can least afford to play.

If gambling is immoral and the state ought to get out of it, state laws that legalize bingo games ought to be repealed. Although an innocuous form of gambling, bingo is still gambling. It involves the exchange of money for a chance to win a prize or more money.

Revenues raised from bingo games go to charitable causes in countless communities around the state. Revenues raised from a lottery would help defray the tax burden on every Virginian. How are the two pursuits significantly different? They aren't.

Some say drinking whiskey, smoking and dancing on Saturday night are immoral, yet the state hasn't outlawed dancing and it even sanctions drinking and smoking through taxes. How would revenues from a lottery be any more tainted than those generated by the sales of alcohol and tobacco products? They wouldn't.

Some critics say a lottery would increase violent crime. How so? How, pray tell, would the deposit of a couple of dollars every so often on chance of winning a couple of thousand raise the state's violent crime rate? Would lottery participants go on a murderous rampage when they find out they have lost? Would the disappointed losers sack the village, committing arson and rape? Of course they wouldn't.

Lottery opponents who raise the violent crime issue are confusing the Hollywood gangland association of gamblers and horse tracks in states that allow pari-mutuel betting. And while I'll concede that the variables involved in horse racing raise the potential for criminal activity (lying, cheating and stealing by thugs who hang around the track), I wouldn't fear a significant increase in violent, crime even with pari-mutuel betting.

The specter of a lottery increasing violent crime is filled with drama, but it has little substance and should be dismissed for the smoke screen it is. I simply don't buy the argument that tries to link a lottery to an increase in violent crime.

To those who argue that poor families will be hurt most by a lottery, I say fiddlesticks. Poor families are going to watch their meager income more closely than those who have an extra dollar or two to play. And those lottery-created gambling addicts that opponents say would be ruined are already with us. Instead of betting the family farm on a lottery, they are doing so in a neighborhood poker game or on numbers rackets or betting on teams in professional or college sports.

The only antidotes I know for a severe case of lottery fever is the purchase of an instant lottery card or a card imprinted with a series of numbers in a "lotto" game. Unfortunately none of the drugstores in Virginia are allowed to dispense either.

If the fever gets too high, I'll have to go over to West Virginia or up to Maryland. The assembly could forestall that trip by apportion of O'Brien's lottery. I'm betting such a move would help the State. Can this potential for state revenue be ignored much longer?

Kill Lottery in Infancy
By Ray L. Garland

RICHMOND—The Capitol is quiet now: The great activist 1987 General Assembly is history. Let us be thankful, at least, that the lottery bill was passed.

That's not because I favor what I believe will become an infernal nuisance, but because 1987 represents probably the last best hope to strangle the beast in its cradle. The people of Virginia will be afforded that opportunity in November, when the question will be placed on the ballot.

All polls indicate a substantial majority of Virginians favor a state lottery, but such polls can be deceptive.

For one thing, they canvass all potential voters, and make no distinction between likely and unlikely voters.

Under normal circumstances, the 1987 turnout (for state legislators, county supervisors and constitutional officers) would be the smallest in the four-year election cycle.

It must be quickly said, of course, that the presence of the lottery issue on the ballot will undoubtedly swell the turnout.

Few things succeed in America until they have taken on the character of modern big business serving a national market. Lotteries are now big business, with slick trade publications, lobbyists and trade associations.

Twenty-five states, embracing well over half the population of the country, now have lotteries. Others are sure to join. In only one state, North Dakota, have voters rejected a lottery.

I've said it before, but it bears repeating: In a lottery, every time a dollar changes hands eight times it has been swallowed by overhead.

That's the effect of the 12–15 percent of ticket sales taken off the top to run the gaudy show and keep the suckers coming.

If Virginia gets the lottery, understandably, most retailers will want to act as agents. They will get a 4–5 percent commission for their trouble, which should translate to some $30 million a year.

The state agency responsible will have administrative costs in the range of $15 million. With advertising, the sky's the limit, of course, but sales will be directly proportional to promotion. It's nonsense to believe you can have a successful lottery without intense and constant bombardment of the consumer.

Every newspaper, billboard company, ad agency, radio and television station in the state—and the District of Columbia—will be angling for a piece of the advertising budget, sure to be in the range of $35 million a year.

The pro-lottery forces start with a popular majority and need only to maintain support with upbeat ads showing that even losers will be winners as benefactors of suffering humanity.

The lottery industry nationwide, consisting of many large firms, can certainly supply necessary campaign funds and expertise, but they must avoid the appearance of trying to buy the state.

In fact, such firms will likely be the only real source of funds for pro-lottery forces. I just can't see the average Joe kicking in twenty bucks to Give Us Lotto League.

Anything less than a million dollar campaign would be tempting fate. Double that and you have a more realistic figure. The industry would get it back the first year.

To come from behind, the anti-lottery forces must do more. They will likely have more willing workers at the grassroots, but they will need at least $2 million—and ought to be able to raise it. There should be 30,000 people in this state, properly solicited, willing to give an average of $50 to stop the lottery.

But the anti-lottery campaign will also need a sophisticated media message. If the issue is presented as a morality play (good v. evil) it will likely fail. Let the pastors stay with their flocks and make sure they get to the polls.

Time is short. The anti-lottery forces must quickly mobilize, and under astute leadership: The choice of commanding general and ad agency will be critical. They must see this as a political campaign, not a merchandising operation. The people chosen to lead must have a record of success in big-time political campaigns.

And media wizardry won't be enough: It must be joined to an old-fashioned get-out-the-vote effort at the grassroots backed by well-organized phone banks and targeted mail. Properly led, the churches can supply the foot soldiers of this crusade.

The presence of the lottery on the ballot will mean this is a highly unpredictable election for the General Assembly.

That it will increase the turnout substantially can't be doubted.

Who will benefit can't be foretold, but conservative-minded voters should be flocking to the polls in record numbers for an off-off year election. Many others, of course, who normally take scant interest in state politics will be flocking as well.

Early assumptions are that the lottery will triumph, but I wouldn't be too sure. People haven't focused on it yet, and the polls are counting many who will not vote unless powerfully motivated by hard and sophisticated effort.

For Comic Relief, Check Out the Lottery Bill Debate
By Steve Clark
Richmond Times Dispatch

Each time the Virginia General Assembly gathers in Richmond, an observer can count on a few scenes of comic relief. My vote for best comedy of the current session goes to the debate over a proposed state-operated lottery.

This little play is full of sidesplitting humor.

Last week, for example, I laughed until I cried at a comment by Del. J.W, "Billy" O'Brien Jr. the Virginia Beach Democrat who is sponsoring a bill that would let Virginia voters say yes or no to a state-run lottery.

Don't call it a "lottery bill," O'Brien said. Call it a "voluntary tax" bill.

It's a numbers game

A voluntary tax? That's marvelous. It's even funnier than President Reagan calling a tax on gasoline a "users' fee."

Let us be frank about what a state-controlled lottery is. It is a legitimate numbers game. You pick a number, and the state sells it to you for a small price. It is not a tax. It is a bet. You are betting the number you picked will win. If it does, you win a large sum of money and you feel very good. If it doesn't win, which is a distinct possibility, you have lost money and you feel miserable.

What's really funny is that if you buy a number from your barber or your butcher, the state calls it gambling and has the authority to arrest you.

But O'Brien's comment was not half as funny as the one by Ted Bowman, an "expert witness" who accompanied O'Brien to a meeting of the House General Laws Committee last week. Bowman is marketing director for a company that handles lotteries in Delaware, Pennsylvania, and Maryland. With a straight face, he told the legislators: "In state lotteries, there are no losers. Only non-winners for the day."

That one broke me up. I know what Bowman meant. He was trying to say that, since profits from a state numbers game go into the state's coffers, taxpayers who don't hit the number shouldn't feel like losers because they are helping themselves indirectly.

OK. But tell somebody who has lost a couple of bucks a day on lottery tickets for a year that he is not a loser, just a non-winner, and he's going to throw his dead lottery tickets in your face.

Proponents of the proposed lottery bill aren't the only stars in this little comedy. These clergymen who are indignant about the proposed lottery are kind of funny, too.

Now, don't get me wrong. I'm not laughing at what the clergymen are saying about a lottery. They are correct in calling a lottery a form of gambling. They are correct in saying that a lottery is a target for fraud. One of the facts of life is that large sums of money will catch the attention of thieves.

However, the clergymen deserve a laugh in this little comedy for things they are not saying about the history of lotteries. They are not telling us about all the church steeples that have been raised and all the sanctuaries that have been built in this country with money made from lotteries, or, "raffles," as the church folk prefer.

History lesson

Yesterday, at another meeting of the House General Laws Committee, an estimated 50 Virginia clergymen showed up to oppose O'Brien's proposed lottery. One of them, the Rev. Gwynn Davis, director of Christian life concerns for the Virginia Baptist General Board, gave committee members a brief history lesson about the lottery in America. From 1790 until 1860, he noted, lotteries were legal in 24 states, one of them Virginia.

"However, the lotteries proved to be so susceptible to fraud that by 1833 they were banned in all states except Louisiana," he said.

Mr. Davis, who said he was speaking as an individual and not as a representative of the board, got his information from a book published in 1960 called "Fortune's Merry Wheel: The Lottery in America," by John S. Ezell. Funny thing, Mr. Davis didn't mention anything about Chapter VIII to Ezell's book, which is styled, "Churches and Schools, 1790–1860." Allow me to provide a few excerpts:

"In the United States from 1790 to the Civil War, 47 colleges, approximately 300 lower schools, and 200 church groups were made recipients of lotteries. Churches were heavy beneficiaries of the philosophy that the ends justify the means, seen in the fact that during this 70-year period 14 states granted lotteries for their religious groups...Worthy of note, also, is that, with the exception of the Quakers, every major denomination and most of the minor groups drank from this fount."

Gradually, American church leaders began to disassociate themselves from money-raising lotteries. But, Ezell notes, sometimes they had a difficult time letting indignation get in the way.

"The 'test by fire' was applied in a meeting of the Missionary Society of New York in 1813 when a roguish individual dropped a Union College lottery chance in the contribution box," Ezell writes. "A long discussion ensued on the propriety of retaining it before the practical decision was agreed upon to withhold a decision until after the drawing!"

Unlike their counterparts of those days, today's church leaders seem pretty certain that a lottery is wrong in the eyes of God. So I guess the moral of this comedy is that the professional servants of God today know a lot more about sin than did the professional servants of God 100 or so years ago.

Baliles: 'Let them vote' on lottery

Staff photo by Bob Brown

READY TO SPEAK — Gov. Gerald L. Ba- liles stands before the microphones to de- liver his State of the Commonwealth ad- dress in the House of Delegates chamber. He is flanked by Senate Clerk Jay Shrop- shire (left), Lt. Gov. L. Douglas Wilder.

Give me life, liberty and a "Lottaluck" lottery
By Sam Barnes, September 4, 1991
The Virginian Pilot

A couple of years from now, it'll all be commonplace.

Now that the General Assembly has approved a lottery referendum, it's just a matter of formalities for us to get it passed and then start winning all those millions.

Before long, we'll all be stopping by the nearest convenience store three times a week to plop down a couple of bucks and buy a fresh lottery ticket.

They'll call it something catchy like a "LottaLuck." And who'll be able to turn down the chance to pay just $2 for a "Lottaluck?"

Then every evening we'll rush home to catch the nightly lottery drawing.

On the nightly shows, some guy in a three-piece suit will glibly announce the numbers on the ping-pong balls he just drew from a cage.

Sometimes we'll get two, maybe even three of the numbers right. So close, yet so far! But next time. Next time!

Then every so often there'll come the really big night—the one that will replace the Final Four, the Super Bowl, the seventh game of the World Series on our list of favorite events. The night of the "LottaLuck Million Dollar Miracle!"

That night, someone will achieve the chief end of 20th century man.

Instant riches. Utter greed fulfillment. The power to shun, once and forever, all meaningful labor and engage in the hedonistic lifestyle of a king.

All for nothing more than the price of a $2 ticket.

On these nights, the show will have to be extra special.

I can see it now. This biggest of all events will have to be scheduled on Washington's birthday. The Father of our Country deserves no less.

TV commercials will tout the "Million Dollar Miracle" for weeks in advance.

They'll tie into the Washington's birthday theme by using two talking $1 bills. George 1 and George 2 will get together and waltz down to the nearest convenience store, where they'll spend themselves for a ticket to the "Million Dollar Miracle."

Then suddenly the screen will fill with a million taking dollars, and the two originals will zoom to the foreground to say: "By George, it can happen to you, too!"

"You just can't lose with a LottaLuck!"

On the night of the big drawing, all of Virginia will be on the edge of its seat. The LottaLuck show will have moved, its ping-pong cages to Mount Vernon for the grand event.

The LottaLuck commission will have tried to get the governor to draw the balls that will determine Virginia's first instant millionaire. But he, and every other major elected official, will have refused, saying they will oppose the lottery on moral grounds.

So, for this inaugural event, actors dressed as George Washington and Thomas Jefferson will officiate.

George and Tom will exchange platitudes about the monumental moment they are about to share, allowing that they hadn't felt such a tingle of excitement since their days as revolutionaries.

Then they'll crank up the ping-pong balls to make history again.

As the numbers are popping up, he will be waving a fickle finger across the state, narrowing its sweep gradually as each finger falls into place.

At the instant the final number is up, the finger will swoop to pick a solitary soul.

That soul will be forever changed and so, do doubt, will Virginia.

As they prepare to sign off, George and Tom will embrace and shake hands and muse about the great times to come.

"This is just the beginning," George and Tom will say. "I hear tell that next year we'll be giving away $2 million!"

"Oh boy," George will opine breathly, "I cannot tell a lie: If they'd had LottaLuck back in my day, I'm not sure I would've ever left town long enough to make it to Valley Forge!"

Tom will laugh a knowing laugh and say: "Oh yes you would've George. You were a man with a mission—to present life, liberty and our right to pursue LottaLuck!"

Editorials—Give Lottery a Chance

Some members of Congress feel a national game may be the answer to the national debt.

At least three bills calling for the creation of a national lottery have been introduced in the U.S. House of Representatives recently. A fourth would set up a commission to study establishment of such a lottery.

Predictably, the proposals have been criticized by religious groups strongly opposed to gambling. The idea also draws fire from state lottery associations none too pleased with the prospect of competition.

Who supports a national lottery? The American public, apparently. A 1984 Gallup poll showed 62 percent of those surveyed in a nationwide random sampling approved of the idea, while 26 percent opposed it. Another 12 percent had no position.

Lotteries, of course, are nothing new, not even the idea of a national one. The Continental Congress instituted such a measure in 1776 to raise $10 million to finance Revolutionary War troops. Eventually, the practice was forsaken. Sweepstakes also played a part in the creation of at least three Ivy League schools—Columbia, Dartmouth, and Harvard.

But in the 1950s, the federal government outlawed lotteries, a ban which held until 1975, when Congress granted exemptions for state-run contests.

Today, Washington D.C. and 19 states have lotteries. Missouri and West Virginia will join the list this year. Virginia does not allow lotteries.

Proponents say a national game would raise money to reduce the deficit. Detractors talk about compulsive gambling and claim the poor are the most vulnerable to such appeals.

The money-raising potential is unquestionable. Americans spent more than $8 billion last year on lotteries, netting state coffers $3 billion. It is estimated that a national lottery could raise $10 billion to $30 billion annually, figures from which state lottery associations that fear loss of profits should take some consolation.

As for comparing lottery players to hard-core gamblers, that's not an argument, it's a scare tactic.

Buying a lottery ticket is no more harmful than playing bingo—something rich and poor Americans by the millions do every day with great enjoyment, many under the auspices of their church. Indeed, across the country bingo has probably financed an impressive number of building projects for churches and civic groups.

Americans obviously like lotteries and they will continue to make them financially successful in states where such games are allowed, even if they have to take their money across state borders—as many Virginians do now in Washington and as many will soon do in West Virginia.

Considering the dismal state of the country's finances, Congress should at least name a commission to examine the possible benefits of a national lottery. Give it a chance.

Lottery Bill Compromise Dealt Setback in House
By Dale Eisman, *Times-Dispatch* staff writer

A state lottery bill, which has seemed the closest thing to a sure bet at the General Assembly for weeks, collapsed on the House floor yesterday; its prospects for passage before today's scheduled adjournment appeared no better than even money.

The 62–38 vote against a compromise lottery plan proposed by House and Senate conferees stunned lottery backers. They promised to try to negotiate a new compromise today so state voters can consider the lottery question in a November referendum.

Opponents, meanwhile, suggested that yesterday's vote indicates that the tide of public sentiment is turning against a lottery.

"The public is learning how bad a proposition the lottery is for Virginia," said a beaming Del. William T. Wilson, D-Alleghany.

A red-faced Del. J.W. O'Brien Jr., who has made the lottery bill a personal crusade for most of the last decade, stalked the rear of the chamber after the vote, muttering curses at members who voted to cut off debate on the bill before he had a chance to make his closing argument.

"I'm livid...I'm not going to say anything now because I'm too mad," O'Brien, D-Virginia Beach, told reporters.

"He shouldn't even say that," said Majority Leader Thomas W. Moss Jr., D-Norfolk, standing nearby.

The lottery battle is foremost in a series of House-Senate disputes that threaten to make the last day of the Assembly session a long one. More than two dozen bills, including hotly contested revisions in the state's conflict of interest law, remain in conference committees.

Also still unresolved were bills to:

- Permit limited television coverage of trials in selected state courts.
- Require school administrators to notify the parents of students suspected of using illegal drugs.
- Eliminate exemptions from jury duty enjoyed by doctors, lawyers, police officers and a variety of other groups.
- Permit a spouse found at fault in a divorce to collect alimony.
- Toughen state regulation of solicitations by charities.

The lottery was tripped up yesterday by members who were among the 61–39 majority supporting it when it passed the House several weeks ago. They were turned, several said, by the conferees' adoption of Senate suggestions that there be no legal restrictions on how the lottery is advertised.

Unfettered lottery advertising would "change how we do things in Virginia," argued Del. William S. Moore Jr., D-Portsmouth. A succession of television ads, billboards and other appeals would encourage everyone, including children, to gamble, he said.

YES: A Needed Non-tax Way to Generate Revenue
By Landon L. Taylor

THE LOTTERY will be good for Virginia, not just by providing our citizens with an additional form of entertainment but as a non-tax revenue-generating vehicle. The Senate Finance Committee, after extensive study of the issue, has determined that Virginia can expect to net $201 million annually from the lottery.

While this will not solve all of the future financial needs of the commonwealth, it will go a long way to meet them. This is more money than raising the state sales tax .5 cents would generate. According to the State Taxation Department, using 1987 taxable sales figures, a half-penny increase in the state sales tax would raise $190 million.

Despite the recent budget surplus announcement (which most people realize resulted from a one-time federal tax law change), the need for additional revenue in Virginia is evident in almost every department and category in the state. A recent legislative tour came up with $2 billion in capital outlay requests from around the state. The main state library, the building that houses our state archives, was closed for over a month because it would not pass building inspections. We are hard pressed to find the money to build a new one The State Mental Health and Retardation Board recently told us they need $140 million in additional monies for critically needed programs in Virginia. Teachers, law enforcement and fire officials, senior citizens and the handicapped all need more money for their programs. These are just a few of the groups that would benefit from lottery revenues.

Virginians already play the lottery, spending millions of dollars on Maryland, D.C. and West Virginia lottery games. We need to keep those millions of dollars in Virginia for our programs. I'm sure those jurisdictions are pleased as punch that we fund so many of their projects.

We've heard the anti-lottery people claim the lottery is an inefficient way to raise money. Admittedly it is not as efficient as raising taxes, but you have a choice with the lottery and no choice with tax increases.

The opposition says the state shouldn't get into the lottery business. They said the same thing about liquor by the drink and state-run liquor stores. Yet the advent of those two institutions has helped spur our vibrant tourism industry and generated $36 million in profits last year for localities and the state. I saw where some Alexandria officials are opposed to the lottery, but I'll bet they'll be among the first in line to request some of the profits.

The lottery will help retail businesses attract additional customers who will come to their stores to purchase tickets and buy additional merchandise while they are in the building. In addition, the retail vendors will make 5 cents on every dollar of tickets they sell. A recent article in the *Springfield*

Times highlighted a Virginia service station owner who said his business has increased 7 percent since he started offering free Maryland lottery tickets with every fill-up. Stories of similar or greater success can be found throughout the states currently with a lottery.

THE MYTHS ABOUT the poor playing the lottery in disproportionate numbers are just that, myths. Study after study has shown that the majority of players are middle-income ($18,000 to $34,000 a year). The opposition sounds so paternalistic when they say the poor don't have enough common sense to know how often they can buy a lottery ticket. They may not make as much money as some others, but that doesn't mean they are not intelligent.

The Senate Finance Committee notes that the average lottery expenditure per person will be $2.38 a week, or $124.46 per year. The opposition keeps using inflated figures to scare people, and even stoops so low as to say 2,000 children will go to bed without food each night if the lottery passes. Of course they don't tell you that the people playing the lottery in the amounts they use in their "children example" probably can afford to have their meals catered and none of their children will go to bed hungry.

The opposition says a new class of welfare recipients and criminals will be created by the lottery. Interestingly enough, the 6,500 working men and women police officers that deal with crime every day on the streets and are members of the Virginia State Lodge of the Fraternal Order of Police have endorsed the lottery. A survey by the Senate Finance Committee found that only Fairfax County had little to no illegal numbers operations because of the players' easy access to lotteries in D.C. and Maryland.

The opposition finds one or two isolated incidents of misfortune involving a lottery in Pennsylvania, Michigan or New Jersey and touts them as if that is what happens on every block in every locality. They know that is not the case. You can find isolated cases of misfortune with everyone from ministers to sports figures, but that doesn't mean they are all bad.

The bottom line is that the lottery is a question of choice, the right of Virginians to choose if they want a lottery game in the state. If they say yes, they have the right to choose if they ever want to play it. The fact that it will generate $201 million in non-tax revenue for the state and keep millions of Virginia dollars within our borders is icing on the cake.

This is a once in a lifetime opportunity for Virginians to vote on the lottery. On Nov. 3, I hope they exercise their right and vote yes.

(London L. Taylor, a Richmond accountant and Businessman, is state co-chairman of Virginians for the Lottery.)

Lotto's Main Backer Cautious
O'Brien says he won't play
By Jean McNair, September 19, 1988
Associated Press

CHESAPEAKE—Even though he led a sometimes lonely, six-year crusade for a Virginia lottery, Del. J. W. "Billy" O'Brien, Jr. won't be in line when the first lottery tickets go on sale Tuesday.

"I have some reluctance about buying a ticket by virtue of the fact that if I won, somebody would say, "'Hey, it's crooked,'" O'Brien said with a grin. "It would be my luck I would win."

O'Brien, a Virginia Beach Democrat, is feeling good these days as he watches the flood of advertisements for the lottery and the excitement of merchants preparing to sell tickets. He will hand out the first lottery prizes during a ceremony in Richmond at noon Tuesday.

When O'Brien first introduced his lottery bill in 1982, fellow legislators treated it as a joke, he said. Then-Gov. Charles S. Robb laughingly told O'Brien he would sign the bill if it became law. O'Brien said, knowing that the bill would never emerge from the General Assembly.

When O'Brien got the bill through a committee in a subsequent session, he reminded Robb of his promise.

"I don't remember telling you that," O'Brien recalled Robb responding. "He never thought I could get it out of committee."

O'Brien's luck changed after the General Assembly approved an increase in the state sales tax during a special session in 1986. Eager to void more tax increases and aware of voter support for a lottery, the legislators passed a lottery referendum in 1987. The voters overwhelmingly approved the game last November.

"I just think people would rather have a voluntary tax," O'Brien said from the office where he works as an adult career counselor for Chesapeake schools.

"This is a very good source of revenue." O'Brien said he expects the Virginia lottery to generate $400 million to $450 million a year. He comes up with that figure by looking at Maryland, which has a million fewer people than Virginia and reaps $327 million annually from a lottery. He said the Virginia games also should benefit from the state's nearly 500-mile border with North Carolina and Tennessee, which have no lotteries.

Ironically, O'Brien got his idea for the lottery from Maryland legislators who bragged about how much the games earned for their state. Now the Virginia lottery could cost Maryland some ticket buyers who live in northern Virginia.

The Virginia lottery will start with $1 tickets that buyers scratch off to see if they have won. Prizes will range from $2 to $5,000.

156

To keep customers interested, O'Brien said the state will have to move quickly into higher-stakes games in which players pick up to six winning numbers.

Opponents' Efforts Fall Just Short
By BILL BYRD, Staff writer
Virginian Pilot

RICHMOND—By a razor-thin margin, the Senate on Tuesday said Virginia should set up a state-operated lottery if the voters agree to the idea in a referendum this fall.

During a tense session marked by emotional attacks on gambling, the Senate voted, 21–19, to approve a bill that could pave the way for a Virginia lottery. The bill, establishing a lottery commission to run state-sponsored games, would take effect if the voters endorse the lottery on Nov. 3.

The measure received solid support from senators from Hampton Roads and Northern Virginia, but faced fierce opposition from rural members.

"I say to you...that what we're doing here today is as wrong as wrong can be," said Sen. Howard P. Anderson, D-Halifax. "I don't know any issue that's come along during my 30 years in the legislature that I've had more concerns about than this."

With the commission measure proved, a second bill ordering a public vote on the lottery was passed by a more comfortable margin, 27–13.

Supporters of the lottery greeted the votes with relief. Unsure they had enough votes for passage, the proponents had spent a "very nervous" Tuesday morning trying to shore up support, said Sen. Charles L. Waddell, D-Loudon.

"I had the hell scared out of me," said the lottery commission bill's sponsor, Sen. William E. Fears, D-Accomac, after his measure squeaked through. Asked how he felt, Fears had a one-word reply: "Shaky."

"Was this a big step!" Fears exclaimed, noting the General Assembly's long-standing opposition to lotteries. "All the old-timers were rolling in their graves!"

Although major victories for the supporters of the lottery, Tuesday's votes do not mark the end of the General Assembly's debate.

The House of Delegates approved its version of lottery legislation last week. Both the House and Senate bills set up commissions to run statewide gambling and call for the referendum, but they also differ in several ways. The House bill, for example, would restrict lottery advertising.

Photo Photo

Supporters were optimistic that a conference panel could work out the differences. "The differences aren't all that great," Fears said. "Somehow, they'll find a way to get the referendum to the public this fall."

Fears said, however, that he might try to keep the issue out of a conference panel by asking the House to relent and accept the Senate version.

Uncertainty surrounded the Senate when it convened at noon. After a streak of victories in the Assembly this year, lottery supporters had conceded Monday that the vote would be close.

"We thought we had 21 or 22 votes," Waddell said. Everyone was worried that some of us might switch at the last minute." Lottery supporters recalled that similar legislation died on a 20–20 vote during September's special session.

Opponents of state-run gambling launched emotion attacks during Tuesday's hour-long debate. They asserted that a lottery would victimize the poor, lead to more crime and damage Virginia's reputation.

"The lottery is nothing more than a state-operated numbers racket," said Sen. Wiley F. Mitchell Jr., R-Alexandria, one of the few Northern Virginians to oppose it. "It appeals to greed, to getting something for nothing. What we don't see is the hundreds of thousands of dollars it bleeds from the economy. It's a fraud against the people, misleading and deceptive."

Mitchell said that only 25 percent to 30 percent of the proceeds from a lottery would end up in the state's general fund; the rest would pay for prizes, administration and advertising. "The money would go for groceries, for rent, for doctors' bills," he said. "It is an economic hemorrhage from people who can least afford to pay it."

Anderson also said the lottery would harm the poor.

"It's the most regressive of regressive taxes," he said. "It goes against the very people that it's intended to help." He noted that many state lottery promotions are designed to sell tickets in lower-income areas.

Arguing that a lottery would harm the state's reputation, Anderson said he was sure many of the legislators who sat in the Senate in years past would take a dim view of the proposals.

"I would think that they would simply raise their eyebrows one time and down the drain it would go."

Another opponent, Sen. Dudley J. Emick, D-Fincastle, said a lottery referendum this fall would jeopardize legislators' chances for re-election. Voters opposed to the lottery will be drawn to the polls and will be eager to punish lawmakers who supported the bills, he said.

"What you're doing is guaranteeing a lot of turnout," Emick said. "What you're doing is increasing the electorate and bringing out people who are mad at you."

All 140 Assembly seats will be up for election this fall.

Fears, however, argued that the lottery could pump hundreds of millions of dollars into the treasury.

"I hope the rest of you will have the nerve to take a little bit of a risk to raise some money for the commonwealth," he said. "Are we going to be the last (state) to come into the 21st century?"

The lottery is the Assembly's only alternative for raising more money, he said. "Raising taxes is anathema to all the people out there in the boondocks," he said. "Are you ready to raise taxes to meet the needs of the commonwealth, or do you want an alternate source the public will accept?"

Fears said he sympathized with the rural legislators who almost doomed his bill.

"The rural boys are scared to death of it," he said. "They're under tremendous pressure in those Bible Belt areas."

All five South Hampton Roads senators—Norfolk Democrats Peter K. Babalas and Stanley C. Walker, Portsmouth Democrat Johnny S. Joannou, Chesapeake Democrat William T. Parker, Virginia Beach Democrat Clarence A. Holland and Virginia Beach Republican A. Joe Canada Jr.—supported the two lottery bills.

Lottery Wins in Virginia by 57 Percent
But Montgomery County Rejects Gambling Plan
By staff and wire reports
Richmond Times Dispatch

After a decade of trying, supporters of a state lottery have tasted victory as Virginia voters turned out in large numbers to support a referendum to use the games to raise money.

But the lottery was defeated in Montgomery and Pulaski counties and the City of Radford. Montgomery voters rejected the lottery 7,752 against to 5,305 for—a 59.3 percent no vote. In Pulaski voters turned it down 4,215 to 3,786. Radford voters rejected it 1,747 to 1,411.

More than half of the state's 2.66 million registered voters showed up at the polls Tuesday with temperatures in the 70s to decide the only statewide issue on the 1987, ballot. In Montgomery County, 55.24 percent of the registered voters cast ballots on the lottery.

Rev. Robert Blinn, organizer of the Montgomery County Virginians Against State-Sponsored Gambling, said he was disappointed in the outcome.

"We tried to do the best we could in Montgomery County, we knew the lottery would have a plurality in the north and east," Blinn said. "Our next battleground will be to try and keep in place the restrictions on advertising the lottery that the General Assembly put in place in 1987," Blinn said.

The Assembly has limited advertising of the lottery to a low-key instructional type, Blinn said, in order to avoid using emotional appeals to sell the lottery.

"We don't feel that the public is aware yet of the seriousness of the hidden costs associated with the lottery," Blinn said.

After the lottery was assured of victory, Del. J.W. "Billy" O'Brien of Virginia Beach, who has pushed the issue in the General Assembly for several years, held a state Capitol press conference to celebrate the achievement.

"I'm elated and feel a great sense of accomplishment, having spent eight years of my life working toward this goal," O'Brien said.

With 1,948 of 1,976 precincts reporting, the lottery had 780,642 "yes" votes to 595,031 "no" votes. The issue passed 57 percent to 43 percent.

Votes in suburban Washington, D.C. areas of northern Virginia and in the Richmond-to-Tidewater urban corridor carried the referendum. It was rejected in rural south side, western and southwest areas of the state. In the 2nd congressional District of Virginia Beach and Norfolk, the lottery was a 2–1 winner.

Jeff Gregson of Free Enterprisers Against the Lottery conceded defeat about 9:30 p.m., some 2_ hours after the polls closed.

Approval of the referendum means a state lottery law passed at the 1987 legislative session last winter will take effect Dec. 1. The law creates a state

Lottery Department to operate the games. An "instant" lottery could begin in about 90 days.

Supporters of the lottery said it could raise about $200 million for the state treasury. The lottery law does not designate how lottery revenues would be spent.

Lottery opponents appeared to have the momentum in the final weeks of the referendum campaign. A *Richmond Times-Dispatch* poll published Sunday showed 58 percent for the games to 35 percent against, with 7 percent undecided. But that was down from a mid-September poll in the newspaper showing 66 percent for to 29 percent against.

Kenneth W. Storey of Virginians for the Lottery credited pro-lottery leaders such as Sen. William E. Fears, D-Accomack, for helping to overcome an erosion of support for the issue as the campaign neared its end.

Opponents raised more than twice as much money as supporters during the campaign.

Virginia will become the 28th state to have a lottery. Neighboring Maryland and West Virginia, as well as the District of Columbia, also have lotteries.

Lottery wins in Virginia by 57 percent

But Montgomery County rejects gambling plan

By staff and wire reports

After a decade of trying, supporters of a state lottery have tasted victory as Virginia voters turned out in large numbers to support a referendum to use the games to raise money.

But the lottery was defeated in Montgomery and Pulaski counties and the City of Radford. Montgomery voters rejected the lottery 7,752 against to 5,305 for — a 59.3 percent no vote. In Pulaski voters turned it down 4,215 to 3,786; Radford voters rejected it 1,747 to 1,411.

More than half of the state's 2.66 million registered voters showed up at the polls Tuesday with temperatures in the 70s to decide the only statewide issue on the 1987 ballot. In Montgomery County, 55.24 percent of the registered voters cast ballots on the lottery.

Rev. Robert Blinn, organizer of the Montgomery County Virginians Against State-Sponsored Gambling, said he was disappointed in the outcome.

"We tried to do the best we could in Montgomery County, we knew the lottery would have a plurality in the north and east," Blinn said.

"Our next battleground will be to try and keep in place the restrictions on advertising the lottery that the General Assembly

More election results on Pages 3A, 8A, 9A

put in place in 1987," Blinn said.

The Assembly has limited advertising of the lottery to a low-key instructional type, Blinn said, in order to avoid using emotional appeals to sell the lottery.

"We don't feel that the public is aware yet of the seriousness of the hidden costs associated with the lottery," Blinn said.

After the lottery was assured of victory, Del. J.W. "Billy" O'Brien of Virginia Beach, who has pushed the issue in the General Assembly for several years, held a state Capitol press conference to celebrate the achievement.

"I'm elated and feel a great sense of accomplishment, having spent eight years of my life work-

See LOTTERY, page 8A

Wednesday, November 4, 1987, The

AP Photo

Del. Billy O'Brien, D-Virginia Beach, flashes victory signs after a news conference at the Capitol in Richmond Tuesday when the victory of the lottery was assured. O'Brien has been the chief proponent of the lottery for the last six years in the General Assembly.

LOTTERY

continued from page 1A

ing toward this goal," O'Brien said.

With 1,948 of 1,976 precincts reporting, the lottery had 780,642 "yes" votes to 595,031 "no" votes. The issue passed 57 percent to 43 percent.

Votes in suburban Washington, D.C. areas of northern Virginia and in the Richmond-to-Tidewater urban corridor carried the referendum. It was rejected in rural southside, western and southwest areas of the state. In the 2nd congressional District of Virginia Beach and Norfolk, the lottery was a 2-1 winner.

Jeff Gregson of Free Enterprisers Against the Lottery con-

ceded defeat about 9:30 p.m., some 2½ hours after the polls closed.

Approval of the referendum means a state lottery law passed at the 1987 legislative session last winter will take effect Dec. 1. The law creates a state Lottery Department to operate the games. An "instant" lottery could begin in about 90 days.

Supporters of the lottery said it could raise about $200 million for the state treasury. The lottery law does not designate how lottery revenues would be spent.

Lottery opponents appeared to have the momentum in the final weeks of the referendum campaign. A Richmond Times-Dispatch poll published Sunday showed 58 percent for the games

to 35 percent against, with 7 percent undecided. But that was down from a mid-September poll in the newspaper showing 66 percent for to 29 percent against.

Kenneth W. Storey of Virginians for the Lottery credited pro-lottery leaders such as Sen. William E. Fears, D-Accomack, for helping to overcome an erosion of support for the issue as the campaign neared its end.

Opponents raised more than twice as much money as supporters during the campaign.

Virginia will become the 28th state to have a lottery. Neighboring Maryland and West Virginia, as well as the District of Columbia, also have lotteries.

Delegate Billy O'Brien – "V" for Victory. Staff photo by Bob Brown, *Richmond Times Dispatch*.

O'Brien Relishes a Personal Victory
By THOMAS BOYER, Staff writer
Virginian Pilot

RICHMOND—If there was an election-night turning point for J.W. "Billy" O'Brien, it came at 8:55 p.m., when someone told him that the lottery was winning big in Lynchburg, home of the Rev. Jerry Falwell.

"Oh!" O'Brien said with a laugh, a deep snort of a laugh. "Oh!" The man who would like to be remembered as the George Washington of the Virginia lottery flashed his biggest, widest grin of the night.

He said nothing, but the meaning of his smile was clear. The Democratic delegate from Virginia Beach had written two statements to read at a press conference in the Capitol media room, one if the lottery won, another if it lost. Now he knew which he would use.

The sponsor of the lottery law read his victory speech, calling Tuesday "a great day for democracy" and relishing a moment he had sought for six years.

"There were times when I mentioned the lottery that not many people up here would listen to me. But that people listened to me is evident by the vote today," he read. "To say the least, I am elated and feel a great sense of accomplishment, having spent many years of my life working toward this goal."

By now, his expression had turned somber, distressing one TV cameraman. "Billy, can you give us a victory sign?" he asked.

As the cameras clicked, O'Brien complied, raising both arms, first making V-for-victory signs with his fingers, then turned thumbs up, flashing that grin again, the smile that has become a symbol of the Virginia lottery.

Then he acknowledged that his lottery crusade still isn't over. He said he would introduce a bill to remove restrictions on advertisements "inducing" people to gamble. And O'Brien said he would like to see lottery revenues earmarked to help pay for prescription drugs for the elderly.

O'Brien's own re-election to the House of Delegates was never in question: He was unopposed. But when he arrived at the Capitol, he had the look of a candidate in for a long, tough fight. He had skipped dinner—too nervous to eat, his aides said. And though the early results showed the lottery winning solidly in urban areas, O'Brien refused to start celebrating.

"I don't know, could be 2 or 3 o'clock in the morning" before the result was known, he said.

In the past year, O'Brien's romance with the game often turned bittersweet and paradoxical. No one wanted the lottery with more passion, yet at times he seemed adept at hurting his cause with unwitting blunders.

Last winter, as lottery bills were making their way through the General Assembly, he wanted to show his fellow House members how the games could contribute to the public good.

So O'Brien showed them a Maryland Lottery television commercial that maintained—wrongly, as it turned out—that lottery revenues bought helicopters to rescue lost children.

Many House members, repelled by the ad, demanded limits on lottery advertising.

Several months later, he almost got the pro-lottery campaign derailed by asking for a $180-a-day salary from campaign donations to travel around the state advocating the game. O'Brien, who had taken an unpaid leave from his job as a school counselor in Chesapeake, said he merely wanted to recover lost earnings, but his request created the appearance that he was trying to profit from the movement.

Even the biggest financial backer of the pro-lottery movement, Georgia-based lottery ticket producer Scientific Games Inc., wanted him out. In an emotional press conference, he withdrew from the campaign and went back to his job.

Ken Thorson, first Director of Virginia Lottery, left, and Delegate Billy O'Brien, right.

It Was Day of Anticlimaxes for O'Brien
By Bill McKelway, *Richmond Times-Dispatch* staff writer
11-04-1987

As polling booths shut down yesterday, a rumpled-looking man carrying a briefcase emerged from the shadows of the Capitol grounds.

"There was supposed to be a place where returns were coming in," J.W. "Billy" O'Brien Jr., explained as he moved into the silent halls of the Capitol, pulling at one unyielding doorknob after another.

He finally made his way over to the General Assembly Building, where he found a corner office in the otherwise dark structure where some House clerks were listening to returns.

O'Brien, 58, spent the evening there.

In the end, the lottery's most loyal proponent was one of the least conspicuous.

He kept asking everyone, "Have you heard anything about the lottery?"

It was a day of anticlimaxes for the Democratic lottery booster from Virginia Beach. In his early years in the legislature, he watched one lottery bill after another fall by the wayside and then, beginning in 1982, saw the same thing happen to his own efforts.

Yesterday all that changed by a margin of 14 percent.

"To say the least, I am elated and feel a great sense of accomplishment," O'Brien finally summoned the confidence to say at 9:20 and gave a victory sign.

"I don't think it's going to change Virginia; it's going to make it a better state."

But the limelight of this day pretty much bypassed O'Brien, whose pro-lottery orations usually fell on deaf ears of fellow politicians.

What for O'Brien has always seemed a "workingman's rainbow" for others seemed the advocated ruination of a state.

O'Brien voted yesterday morning; spent the day on the job as an assistant school administrator in Chesapeake; and then drove to Richmond to listen to voting results.

"I've got a statement for if we lose and one for if we win," he said earlier in the evening. I'll read one or the other and then be on my way."

Both statements began identically, celebrating the vote as "another great day in the commonwealth...."

O'Brien had no plans to show up at victory parties and spokesmen for Virginians for the state Lottery said they didn't expect to see him at headquarters yesterday.

Part of the reason is that O'Brien, in some minds, tried to cash in earlier that most on the vast wealth that the lottery supposedly provides. News reports in the summer that he had asked a promotional company, Scientific

Games Inc., for a daily fee to stump for the lottery helped lead to his decision not to take an active role in the campaign.

Since then, O'Brien, who earlier foresaw a visible role for himself in the move toward making Virginia the 29th lottery state, has been as silent as the prairie breezes of Kansas, his native state.

Higher-ups in the lottery campaign told him he had gotten too personal, O'Brien said last night. In effect, he became a pariah of the cause he had carried almost alone for nearly a decade.

"I was too emotionally involved, I guess," he said last night.

It was like that in the general Assembly, too, where O'Brien's persistence on behalf of the lottery was fueled by the feeling that the people of the state had been left in the cold by a too-fatherly legislature for too long.

O'Brien's lottery bills over the years promised to cure an accountant's lexicography of financial ills, could materialize after a moment's whimsy and always drew a crowd.

"With a reedy voice, O'Brien invokes images of sugar plums," a reporter wrote once. He said after every defeat that things were "looking better all the time."

Last night, when it was over, O'Brien predicted that the first lottery ticket could go on sale by April. "I hope they sell it to me." His legislative agenda will include more educational issues now, he said, but not before he makes an effort to rid the lottery law of provisions limiting advertising.

Preventing advertising "is an exercise in futility," said O'Brien, a man who knows the feeling well.

SENIOR REPORT
Seniors Could Become Big Winners in Lottery
By Robin Ben-Shimeon, Correspondent
Virginian Pilot

No matter how you scratch it, every state lottery ticket will be a winner for Virginia's senior citizens if a proposed bill by Del J.W. "Billy" O'Brien Jr. becomes law.

The bill, which he plans to introduce in January, would allow lottery proceeds to be used to reduce medical prescription-costs for older residents.

O'Brien says that by living longer senior adults are faced with thousands of dollars per year in prescription costs that threaten to send aging residents and their families to the "poor house."

"I think we as a society shouldn't bankrupt them just so they can live a little longer," O'Brien explained, adding that those who are living on pensions and other retirement income, and who do not qualify for Medicaid, are caught in a bind. Often, he noted, seniors take several types of prescription drugs per day for a variety of ailments.

Pharmacy Assistance Contract for the Elderly, a similar program, is already in place in 13 states, O'Brien said. Under the plan, seniors age 65 and older and whose income is less than $15,000 per year would be eligible to purchase prescriptions at a reduced rate, he said.

Just how much that rate would be has not yet been determined.

"I think society owes these people some consideration," he explained, noting that the plan would help relieve those on fixed incomes whose prescription bills alone can total several hundred dollars per month.

O'Brien, who spearheaded the drive to get a lottery established in Virginia, said he hopes the proceeds will be used to fund "flesh and blood (programs), not bricks and mortar."

The lottery money is currently going into the general fund until the legislature decides where the money will be allocated.

The proposal is still being drafted, O'Brien said, because he is trying to determine how the catastrophic health bill recently passed by Congress will affect seniors and their soaring medical costs. He's also trying to determine how much of the lottery funds would be needed to fund the program.

The "big money" lotto games won't begin for about another six months, he estimated, perhaps after the legislative session has recessed. By law, he said, before lottery money can be appropriated, it must already be deposited in the bank. At this time, he said, it is difficult to determine how much money the lottery will actually raise.

He will discuss his prescription plan Oct. 25 in Richmond at a meeting of a subcommittee appointed by the governor to study various health needs.

O'Brien said he will introduce the bill in January and it will be reviewed by the Appropriations Committee.

He said he will try to convince the legislature to choose one county or city, perhaps Virginia Beach, O'Brien said, to serve as a pilot project for the program.

But, he added, it could take up to two years before the prescription program gets under way.

He suggested that seniors speak out and let the legislators know what's on their minds.

One who is not afraid to do that is Virginia Beach senior citizen activist Madeline Nevala. She plans to work with local members of the American Association of Retired Persons and the Mayor's Committee on Aging to form a coalition to see that at least a portion of the lottery money is used to help senior citizens, as well as education.

"If you want it, you've got to work for it," says Nevala, who also serves on the Southeastern Virginia Area wide Model Program's board of directors. She also would like to see lottery money used for the purchase of vans to provide transportation for seniors and to build a centralized senior citizen center in Virginia Beach.

That's not out of the question, she said, considering what's been done in other states.

Sylvia Hubbard, 68, of Quakertown, Pa., said the lottery in her state has afforded seniors a variety of opportunities, from reduced medical prescriptions and taxicab fares to tax rebates.

"We love it. We're very pleased and we use it [the lottery provisions for senior citizens] whenever we can," she said. Because of the lottery, seniors, age 65 and older, only pay $4 per prescription, and they pay only $10 per year for license plate tags.

The State Grubbery
01-03-1991
Richmond Times Dispatch

Have a dollar or two left over after your Christmas shopping and don't know how to burn it? Fear not. The folks over at the state Grubbery, er., Lottery Department will find a way to dispose of it for you.

Fresh from starting a second weekly Lotto drawing on Halloween and sweetening the pot for retailers by $5,000 if they sell a winning ticket, the department is continuing its relentless quest to paper the whole state with losing lottery tickets.

The next step may be to go in cahoots with the state government's other monopoly and peddle lottery tickets at the state-owned liquor stores in Northern Virginia. The Lottery Board has agreed to study the idea. It seems the department has trouble finding retailers in Northern Virginia who think turning their businesses into casinos for the state is worth the bother and grief. Maybe those folks up there haven't become demented from breathing all those auto fumes after all.

The patron saint of the state's sucker's game, Del. J. W "Billy" O'Brien, D-Virginia Beach, says the state will mix monopolistic gambling and booze "over my dead body." Hey, Billy, it's a little late to be getting religion, isn't it?

But that's not all: The lottery wizards also plan to start installing some 400 automatic ticket-vending machines in Northern Virginia by next spring. The machines would be placed in office buildings, grocery stores and news-stands. Can anyone seriously doubt that if vending machines and then sales in ABC stores become established in the northern provinces, the rest of the state will follow shortly?

And there's still more grubbiness: The lottery plans to pump an extra $3.5 million into advertising designed to extract those final dollars out of your pockets.

What's next? Will the state adopt payroll deductions, a la the United Way, for lottery purchases? Will DMV offices peddle lottery tickets? Will lottery vending machines be installed in restrooms?

Whatever the next gambit may be, one may be sure that ever-more-grubby ways to promote the state monopoly are just down the road. The problem is that once a state resorts to this slimy way of raising revenues, it must scramble constantly to contrive new lures to keep the revenues flowing in.

For people grow weary of being snookered out of their last dollars, especially when they can ill afford to part with them, and so participation in the old games wane. We can hardly wait to see what gimmicks the Grubbery will invent if the economy goes into a deep recession.

Lottery is Object of Many Potshots
By John Goolrick, Columnist
01-13-1991
Richmond Times Dispatch

A blue-collar worker in an old clunker pulls up to a 7-Eleven, pumps three bucks worth of gas into the car, goes inside and pulls out a $20 bill to pay for the gas, a six pack of beer and $5 worth of lottery tickets.

That's the kind of scene that harsh critics of the Virginia state lottery often paint as they charge that this form of state-sponsored gambling preys on those who are least able to afford it.

The immensely successful and popular lottery, a big money maker from the start, is coming in for even more lumps lately for its increasingly aggressive advertising and marketing techniques and because of suggestions that lottery tickets may be sold in state ABC stores.

A recent editorial in the *Richmond Times-Dispatch* leads off: "Have a dollar or two left over after your Christmas shopping and don't know how to burn it? Fear not. The folks over at the state Grubbery, er, Lottery Department, will find a way to dispose of it for you."

The editorial blasted the state for starting a second weekly Lotto drawing and for giving retailers more cash incentives.

It also noted: "The next step may be to go in cahoots with the state government's other monopoly and peddle lottery tickets at the state-owned liquor stores in Northern Virginia...it seems the department has trouble finding retailers in Northern Virginia who think turning their businesses into casinos for the state is worth the bother and grief."

The editorial pointed out that lottery Officials are tentatively planning to install about 400 automatic ticket vending machines in Northern Virginia by spring to boost sales in that region and to spend $3.5 million more on advertising.

There are many different shades of opinion about the state lottery, but little doubt that people of modest economic means play the lottery most. Yet lottery defenders such as Del J.W. "Billy" O'Brien. D-Virginia Beach, who lead the fight for a state lottery, point out that average lottery players spend only a few dollars a week on the pursuit of sudden riches and there is no evidence that lottery playing leads to compulsive gambling.

Not only that, says O'Brien, but at a time the state faces a potential $1.9 billion revenue shortfall, most of the state profits from the lottery are being used to help get the budget back in balance.

If it were not for those revenues, O'Brien argues, "we'd either be facing new taxes or even larger reductions in spending for education, health and other vital areas." Even so, O'Brien still clings to his hope that once the crisis passes, lottery profits can be used for highly visible programs to help the elderly or provide more educational opportunities for young people such as is the case in many other areas.

"I've always called the lottery a voluntary tax," he said, "and as such I think the revenues it generate should go toward things that will have a very favorable public impact."

Suggestions that lottery tickets be sold in state operated liquor stores, said O'Brien, should be ignored.

"I don't think that's the idea of the lottery folks," said O'Brien who believes it may be part of a Virginia ABC Board "hidden agenda" to generate more sales of alcoholic beverages in its stores.

The lottery is doing fantastically well," he noted, "and there's no need to sell tickets in liquor stores...Let's face it, places like 7-Eleven don't make any money on what they get for selling lottery tickets. But if somebody comes in and buys lottery tickets and then buys a 55 cent cup of coffee on which they make 30 cents profit, then it's worth it."

Under that scenario, said O'Brien, declining sales of alcoholic beverages through state stores might be propped up.

O'Brien says he sees nothing wrong with the plan to put automatic lottery machines in Northern Virginia. "People are used to buying things out of machines, I think they will have to be placed where someone can keep an eye on them, but I'm sure that can be done."

With the General Assembly back in session, some long-time opponents of a state lottery will almost surely open fire on what they see as the Lottery Board's stepped up advertising and marketing campaign to sell lottery tickets. Said Del. William J. Howell, R-Stafford, who voted against the lottery, "Everyone knows that you have to find new gimmicks all the time to keep up your lottery sales. We warned about that."

Despite protestations, though, the lottery will stick around for a while. The state has few enterprises that are more successful in these bleak times.

Legislature Looks to Lottery Again for Help with Shortfall
By Mollie Gore, *Richmond Times-Dispatch* staff writer

It didn't get as much attention as the legislature's raid on $535 million in lottery revenues, but the 1991 General Assembly also helped itself to a rainy-day fund at the Virginia Lottery.

An $8 million operating reserve was replaced with a $25 million line of credit, Lottery Director Kenneth W. Thorson told the lottery board yesterday during its regular monthly meeting.

"As you know, the General Assembly was desperately seeking revenues," Thorson said. "They were looking everywhere they could."

Legislators left intact a multi-million-dollar lottery prize reserve fund, though, Thorson said.

In the session that ended Saturday, lawmakers passed a bill letting them spend the first 10 months of lottery revenues each year before the end of that year.

They also put lottery profits from the past two years and the anticipated profits for the first 10 months of this fiscal year into the general fund for operating expenses.

Lottery profits originally were earmarked for construction needs around the state. A $2.1 billion budget shortage sparked a change, however.

Also at yesterday's meetings, finance director Ray Patterson reported that lottery sales are continuing to break records.

In January, total ticket sales topped $75 million—beating the monthly sales record of $65.6 million set in November.

By contrast, sales last January, the month Lotto was introduced, totaled about $40 million.

A 31-day month, a big Lotto jackpot of $11.8 million and the start of a new instant game contributed to the record, Patterson said.

Lottery expenses for January were $4.2 million, or 5.6 percent of the department's sales.

So far this year expenses are 6.3 percent of sales. By law, the lottery keeps expenses within 10 percent of its sales.

Thorson gave board members an overview of how the lottery fared in the legislative session, specifically mentioning opposition to a bill that would have increased the state's take from 35 percent to 40 percent of lottery sales.

Two board members who are former legislators, William F. Parkerson Jr. and H. Dunlop Dawbarn, spoke against the bill when testifying before the Senate Finance Committee.

The lottery has maintained that increasing the state's take would force a decrease in the percent of sales spent on prizes—antagonizing players and cutting ticket sales by 20 percent.

"I think that [the legislator offering the bill] was very well-intentioned," said Harris Miller, a board member representing Northern Virginia. "The evidence was overwhelming that the end result would have been less money."

Thorson also noted that Del. J.W. O'Brien Jr. D-Virginia Beach, and the father of the lottery, is retiring.

"It's meant a lot to us to have the interest that he's shown in the lottery," Thorson said.

Is Va. treasury too dependent on lottery cash?

YOU'VE GOT TO HAND it to Kenneth W. Thorson. He's one heck of a gambler.

Some skeptics thought the Virginia lottery director was overreaching a bit when he decided to launch a midweek Lotto drawing. Players would be too busy driving home from work, worrying about the kids, fixing dinner and the like to drop by the neighborhood store for Lotto tickets on Wednesday, the scoffers said.

They were wrong. Wednesday Lotto got off to a roaring start on Halloween night. Bettors snapped up $1.7 million in tickets in just four days — $1.1 million on Wednesday alone. Previously, with Lotto drawings only on Saturday night, gamblers had plunked down an average of just $200,000 for tickets on Wednesdays.

To top it off, there was even a winner, who walked away with a prize of $1.3 million. "We've been very lucky," said a clearly relieved Paula Otto, the lottery's spokeswoman, after the last-minute burst of sales.

BILL BYRD
INSIDE VIRGINIA

Yes, Lady Luck has smiled on Virginia's lottery. But amid the euphoria over the booming ticket sales — now averaging $60 million a month — a few lonely voices are beginning to ask a troubling question about the state's love affair with the games:

Is the treasury's growing reliance on lottery profits too much of a gamble for Virginia?

The skeptics wonder how far the state will go to keep the money coming in. And they question what would happen if the gambling earnings suddenly took a dive.

Just a year ago, nobody was asking those questions. Then Gov. Gerald L. Baliles had pronounced the lottery an unstable source of revenue. Because he considered it too risky to use the proceeds for routine government operations, Baliles had the General Assembly earmark the profits for building programs. He reasoned that the state would suffer no great loss if some construction projects had to be delayed because of a slump in lottery profits.

As it did to so many of Baliles' plans, the economic downturn ended the lottery-backed construction program. Last year, before Baliles left office, the government quietly began diverting gambling profits to pay for routine government services. In August, Gov. L. Douglas Wilder made a clean break with Baliles. Wilder's plan to use $383 million in lottery earnings to finance state operations formed a key part of his plan to eliminate a $1.3 billion revenue shortfall.

Wilder clearly does not consider the lottery either an unstable or an unreliable source of revenue, and predicted that the shift of the profits to pay for government operations would be "more permanent than not."

"It's just as reliable as the corporate (income) tax," he recently told reporters. "When the money is there, we will use it."

As if to emphasize the role of the lottery in his budget-making, Wilder even paid a late-August visit to a meeting of the lottery's governing board. Baliles had carefully avoided such gatherings.

"We can use it," Wilder quipped when Thorson presented him a mock check for $156.5 million, the agency's earnings for fiscal 1990. "I'd like to thank the Lottery Department for its effectiveness and efficiency."

Amid the torrent of devastating financial news from the Capitol in late summer, Wilder's lottery maneuvers attracted relatively little notice. That's now changing.

One cautionary note is being sounded by Wilder's frequent nemesis, Senate Majority Leader Hunter B. Andrews. In an Oct. 24 letter to members of the Senate Finance Committee, Andrews appeared to take issue with Wilder's assertion that using lottery money for state operations is "more permanent than not."

In his letter, Andrews labeled the shift a "one-time adjustment" that could hinder the Assembly's ability to plan for the future.

"To the extent that we unduly rely on one-time savings, we make preparation of the 1992-94 biennial budget more difficult," Andrews wrote. A briefing paper accompanying the letter noted that Wilder's lottery money "assumes virtual elimination of Virginia's capital outlay program."

Republicans have been more blunt, accusing Wilder of applying subtle pressure on the lottery department to juice up profits. (Both Wilder's office and Thorson strongly deny this.)

"The proceeds of a lottery are so unreliable that using them as a building block in governmental proceedings is irresponsible in any circumstance," complained Del. Frank D. Hargrove of Hanover, chairman of the Assembly's Joint Republican Caucus.

Hargrove predicted the Assembly's Republicans will try to short-circuit Wilder's lottery plans when the legislature convenes in January. Because they're outnumbered by more than two-to-one, it's virtually certain the GOP members will fail unless they pick up the support of a high-ranking Democrat such as Andrews.

That prospect isn't totally inconceivable, but given Wilder's immense clout, it probably isn't likely either.

Anyway, evidence suggests that the hand-wringing about Virginia's gambling dependence is premature at best. Here are a few points from veteran lottery-watchers:

■ There's little likelihood of a lottery profits slump, even in a recession. Lotteries in states such as New Jersey, Ohio and Illinois — states hard-hit by the economic downturn in the early 1980s — continued to soar during the bleak years. "Recession actually helped," said Anne Bloomberg, a spokeswoman for the Ohio state lottery. People who played illicit numbers contests in factories shifted to betting on state games once their plants shut down or they were laid off. Other observers also note that a lottery gives those down on their luck, such as the unemployed, a small ray of hope in an otherwise bleak situation.

■ There's little evidence to back up the "unstable and unreliable" label Baliles and others pasted on the lottery. Charles Clotfelter and Philip Cook, two Duke University professors who have scrutinized American gambling, found little but "rapid growth" in lottery profits during the 1980s.

"The state budget process could count on receiving at least as much real revenue from the lottery each year as it had the preceding year," they wrote in their book, "Selling Hope," published last year.

■ Profits in "mature" lottery states do tend to flatten out after awhile. Virginia's lottery is anything but mature. New games are still being introduced, the gambling market is still expanding. And with each new wrinkle, there's another burst of betting — witness the Halloween night Lotto contest.

■ Most states use lottery money to pay for routine government operations, such as education and health. And the alternative to Wilder's plan is more budget cutting. Few legislators would have the nerve to sacrifice state employees in order to keep the building program humming.

■ Finally, we're not talking about that much money. The $383 million Wilder wants from the lottery now represents just over 1.5 percent of the state's $26 billion budget. Even if the lottery eventually produces $250 million to $300 million a year, it would still provide a small portion of the funds needed to keep the state running. Such earnings might, however, help head off a tax increase — a prospect which strikes fear in the hearts of most legislators.

So it's a good bet that Wilder is right when he predicts that the lottery will have a permanent role in fueling the engine of government. And it's an equally good bet the Virginia Lottery will continue to pump out the profits.

Just ask those who thought Thorson was taking too big a chance with Wednesday night Lotto.

Bill Byrd covers Virginia politics and government from Richmond for The Virginian-Pilot and The Ledger-Star.

Va. Public Schools Get Big Check from Lottery
By Emily Hagedorn, *The Virginian-Pilot*

NORFOLK—Virginia public schools hit it big Friday.

Lottery Executive Director Penelope Kyle presented a $375.2 million check of lottery profits to Lt. Gov. Tim Kaine in the Maury High School foyer.

"Without the lottery, we would be in such tough shape," Kaine said. "I wish, I hope and I pray that the legislature will be as good a partner to education as the Virginia Lottery has."

By law, every penny of the lottery's profits must go to education. The $375.2 million profit from the state's fiscal year that ended June 30 surpassed last year's by $7.5 million.

Kyle attributed the record in part to record-setting sales, coupled with the department reducing operating costs. The lottery sold $1.1 billion in tickets during the fiscal year, she said. That's $27.6 million more than last year. Kyle couldn't say whether the current recession bit into possibly higher profits. In the past, she said, profits haven't been affected by the economy.

Military deployments earlier this year had no real impact on lottery sales in Hampton Roads, Kyle said. The region is one of the largest sales areas in the state, she said.

Operating costs were 6.1 percent of sales. Kyle said 10 percent of sales are earmarked for administrative purposes, but the department voluntarily reduced that to 6 percent to help with the state's budget woes.

The department eliminated eight staff positions, reduced the number of special events and canceled a NASCAR sponsorship, among other things, she said.

Because of the lottery's frugality, $4.5 million more went to the bottom line, Kyle said.

"We could not be more proud of the amount we are turning over to the commonwealth," she said.

Kyle said that officials are negotiating for Texas to join Mega Millions, one of the multi-state games in which Virginia participates. If that happens, profits could be higher with the addition of an 11th state to the game.

"The jackpots will jump quicker and be larger," she said.

During the past fiscal year, scratch tickets accounted for 50 percent of sales, which is up from 31 percent in the 2002 fiscal year.

Tangible prizes with the scratch-off tickets, such as Harley-Davidson motorcycles, have attracted many new customers, she said.

One of these includes Valorie Reese, a sales associate at the Exxon gas station on the corner of Boush and Olney streets.

"I'm trying to win the Corvette," she said, holding up a $5 Corvette Summer scratch card.

Reese, 37, said most people buy scratch cards instead of participating in lottery drawings.

"We only get our crowd when it gets to $100 million," she said. "Only when the stakes are high."

Va. Lottery Still Thriving 15 Years Later
BY Larry O'Dell, Associated Press

It has defied the odds despite restrictions on advertising and economic downturns.

RICHMOND—In its first 15 years of operation, the Virginia Lottery has taken <u>$13 billion out</u> of the pockets of players but has returned more than half of it as prize money. The state also has taken a $4.5 billion cut.

Whether all that is good or bad depends on whom you ask, but this much is certain: The lottery has defied the odds by continuing to thrive despite economic downturns, advertising restrictions and the "jackpot fatigue" that sets in when players lose interest in million-dollar prizes.

"We are an anomaly in the lottery industry," said Penelope W. Kyle, executive director of the Virginia Lottery. "Our sales have not flattened out."

Sales have more than doubled from $409 million in fiscal year 1989 to more than $1.1 billion in the fiscal year that ended June 30. The growth has been steady, with sales increasing in all but three years. Profits have increased from nearly $141 million to just over $375 million.

"We turned over more money to the state this year than we ever expected, and we hope to do the same next year," Kyle said.

The key to continued growth, she said, has been the addition of new games to appeal to two types of players—those who favor the instant results of scratch-off tickets, and the millionaire wannabes who prefer the big jackpots of computerized, Lotto-type drawings.

The only game available on Sept 20, 1988, the lottery's first day, was a scratch game called "Match 3." That has grown to more than 60 scratch games and five online games including the multi-state Lotto South and Mega Millions drawings.

Kyle said that the latest strategy for generating interest in the lottery is emphasizing that profits go to public schools. The tie will be strengthened by the lottery's televised scholastic "Battle of the Brains" competition this school year, she said.

The lottery has become such an accepted fixture in Virginia that memories of the fierce debate that preceded its creation have largely faded. However, opponents of state-sponsored gambling are still out there.

"I haven't changed my thinking about it at all," said former state Del. William T. Wilson of Covington, who was the legislature's most vocal opponent of the lottery. "I still think it's an inappropriate way to produce revenue to run a state."

Lottery supporters portrayed the games as a way to bolster state revenue through a form of voluntary taxation. Opponents argued that many poor people, enticed by unrealistic visions of striking it rich, would gamble away the family's grocery money.

Anti-gambling lobbyist Bill Kincaid acknowledges that there is no evidence that the dire predictions of lottery critics have come true, but he says that's because no studies have been conducted.

"There's got to be some societal and financial consequences, but we don't know what they are," he said. "Government should know what the costs are, but in this case, the state of Virginia does not."

Wilson said that he doesn't need scientific data to support his position.

"I haven't gone out and done a poll, but I've got eyes to see, and I see who's playing the lottery," he said. "People who would normally take that money and buy clothing and food for their family and pay the rent are spending that money on the lottery."

Legislators sought to minimize any potential problems by restricting lottery advertising to such basic information as prize amounts and odds of winning. They also required that tickets include a phone number that players can call for help for gambling addiction.

Critics periodically complained that humorous TV spots featuring the lottery's rumpled, wand-toting "Lady Luck" character went beyond what was allowed by law. Those ads have largely vanished—not because of the complaints, Kyle said, but because of tight finances.

"The governor asked all state agencies to cut back, and that includes us," she said. "Our advertising expenditures have dropped 24 percent from our peak year."

Kyle said that the relatively low number of calls to the hot line for problem gamblers is evidence that the lottery is not as addictive as other forms of gambling, such as sports betting.

"Gamblers aren't interested in games of chance. They want to rely on their skills. There is no skill or knowledge involved in getting six numbers for Saturday night," Kyle said.

Lottery spokesman Ed Scarborough said that the hot line receives about 300 calls a year from people seeking help for themselves or someone else for gambling addiction. About one-third of those are lottery related; the rest concern problems with other forms of gambling, he said.

Most callers are referred to Gamblers Anonymous, a program based on the 12-step model of Alcoholics Anonymous.

From South Norfolk to Norfolk County to Chesapeake, we've compiled a list inside of our city's most influential people. What do you think? Go to our Web site and click on Clipper TalkNet.

Pilot Online
Chesapeake news
www.pilotonline.com/clipper

TOP 10

The names and faces below are just a sampling of the Clipper's Chesapeake people of the century. **PAGE 6**

POLITICS
Marian
Whitehurst

EDUCATION
E.W.
Chittum

A&E
Clarence
Clemons

SPORTS
Ken
Easley

COMMUNITY
Donald
Buckley

POLITICS
Hugo
Owens

EDUCATION
Charles
Brabble

A&E
Doris
Sohr

SPORTS
Billy
O'Brien

COMMUNITY
Dan
Hoffler

State's Public Schools Reap Jackpot as Lottery Profits Top $400 Million
By Larry O'Dell, June 30, 2004
Associated Press

RICHMOND—The Virginia Lottery turned a record profit for the third consecutive year, topping $400 million for the first time since the lottery's inception 16 years ago, officials announced Wednesday.

Penelope W. Kyle, the lottery's executive director, presented a large ceremonial check for $408 million to Gov. Mark R. Warner at a news conference at lottery headquarters.

The Virginia Constitution requires the state to use the money for public schools.

Sales increased 11.1 percent to a record $1.26 billion, the lottery said.

"In many states, lottery profits have started to tail off," Warner said. "Our lottery, through creative marketing and through hard work, has set another record."

Warner praised lottery employees for spending only 5.4 percent of its revenue on operating expenses, the lowest percentage in the agency's history. By law, the lottery can spend up to 10 percent of its revenues on administrative costs.

The only game that showed a decrease was Cash 5, which went from $28.4 million in fiscal 2003 to $28 million last year.

The lottery also set records in prize payouts, $720.2 million and retailer compensation, $70.7 million. Those figures were up 12.9 percent and 12.1 percent, respectively, from the previous year.

The agency's profit easily surpassed the $385 million it had projected for state budget purposes.

RETIREMENT

In the year 1989, Governor Doug Wilder introduced a bill that would allow
a State employee that had worked for the State for 25 years to receive an extra
5 years added to his service under the Virginia Supplemental Retirement
Service (VSRS). The Governor initiated this action because of a small depression and the Commonwealth of Virginia taxation fund was running a deficit.

The supposition was this, if enough of those State employees who were
being paid very high wages would retire, they could be replaced with younger
replacements at much lower salaries and that would bring the State deficit
under control. This procedure would cause the State not to have to raise taxes.

As a member of VSRS, I had served the State for a period of 37 years.
This law would give me 42 years of retirement.

I contacted the VSRS and was informed by them that I could retire
under this law and receive more money than when I was working 10 to 12
hours a day.

On the final day of the session, I made a personal privilege speech
informing the members of the House that I had enjoyed about as much as
I could stand serving with this Assembly, in jest, and that I was resigning
from this position.

I guess you are wondering why I just didn't retire from my position with
the Chesapeake School System and continue serving in the General
Assembly and here is the reason:

The makeup in the Virginia General Assembly at that day and time was
about 75% of the members were lawyers. There was a feeling among these
lawyers that they did not want any retired superintendents or principals from
the VSRS to run against them. I thought that law was unconstitutional, but
doubted that I could change the law, so I retired.

To put this in better perspective, I will now try to present a picture of
my District, which the Democratic controlled General Assembly did not
appreciate my decision to retire.

When the U.S. Supreme Court dictated to the Commonwealth of
Virginia that it shall divide the Commonwealth of Virginia into single mem-
ber Districts of equal population, it created the 83rd District in Virginia
Beach, where my wife, Joyce, and I lived in the Harbor Gate Condominiums

on the Chesapeake Bay. The 83rd District was also one of the most Republican Districts in the Commonwealth of Virginia.

The Republican Party in Virginia said, "We are going to put a Republican in that seat."

They ran a Republican against me three times and my wife and I went door-to-door to every registered voter in the 83rd District and kicked their ass every time. I would go down one side of the street and Joyce would go down the other side. Joyce probably got me more votes that I got myself.

The last time I ran for election, they did not oppose me because of all the money spent and the hard work was not worth the effort to defeat me.

After I retired, the 83rd District elected Republican Leo Wardrup and he has been there ever since.

When the Democratic controlled General Assembly went back into session, they put in a bill to allow members to retire under the VSRS and serve in the General Assembly. It was nicknamed the "Billy O'Brien Bill." Delegate Bob Tata of Virginia Beach and Senator Harry Blevins of Chesapeake are now serving in the General Assembly because of the "Billy O'Brien Bill." The Democratic controlled General Assembly had lost a Democrat because they wouldn't let me retire.

I served 18 years in the General Assembly and this is why I retired. I served my first session in the General Assembly and coached my last year's football team at Great Bridge High School. My team won 5 and lost 5 and I felt I couldn't do both.

My wife served as Secretary in the Engineering Department of the Ford Motor Company in Norfolk, Virginia, for 27 years. I worked at the Chesapeake Adult Education Department.

We both worked 8 hours a day. In the months of August, September, and October, during the election year, we would go door-to-door from 4:00 p.m. till 6:00 p.m. every week day. On Saturday, we went door-to-door from 9:00 a.m. till 12:00 noon.

When I retired, she was the happiest lady in the Commonwealth of Virginia.

First Football Reunion after 26 Years

By Bill Leffler, *Correspondent*
The Virginian Pilot

O'Brien asked all 293 of his former players to attend the October event

CHESAPEAKE—It's going to be the biggest gathering of Wildcats ever.

Billy O'Brien, 70, the winningest football coach in Great Bridge High School history, is planning a reunion of his former players in October.

O'Brien, who coached at Great Bridge from 1955 until 1974, has extended an invitation to the 293 players who wore the green and gold during those 20 years.

During that period, Great Bridge's record was 146–43–11. This included five district championships and one state runner-up finish.

O'Brien got the idea from similar events held at the University of North Carolina, where he played his college ball.

A barbecue at 4:30 p.m., Oct. 6 at Colon Hall Stadium in Great Bridge will start the festivities. Sitting together in a special reserved section, the group then will attend the Great Bridge-Oscar Smith football game.

The next day the ex-players will compete in a golf tournament at Cypress Point in Virginia Beach, followed by a sit-down dinner.

"My speech will be free of charge," quipped O'Brien, who went on to become a state legislator after his coaching days.

The barbecue costs $8, the golf tournament $37 and the dinner $25. Checks should be made payable to the "Friends of Wildcat Football" and sent to O'Brien at 1156 Pond Cypress Drive, Virginia Beach, 23455.

The football game fees have been donated by Wayne Bradshaw.

BILLY O'BRIEN REUNION
Players gather to praise ex-Great Bridge coach
The Virginian Pilot

Twenty-six years after Billy O'Brien hung up his football coaching whistle at Great Bridge High School, more than 140 of his former players came back Home-coming weekend to visit him and recall old times.

They remembered the great rivalries with Princess Anne, Norview, Oscar Smith and Woodrow Wilson high schools, and all the winning teams. After all, the Wildcats did go 146–43–11 under O'Brien, who coached from 1955 to 1974.

They came from as far away as California and Washington to remember how O'Brien always had his team ready to play, how his innovative, motivational ways never wavered in 20 years. He taught lessons for life—to play fair, to arrive on time, to be a leader.

More than 250 players, coaches and supporters and their family members attended the pre-game barbecue, so many that when it came time for kickoff, they couldn't all fit in the bleacher section set aside for them.

The next night, at a reunion dinner, there were 182 guests on hand and 20 that couldn't because Las Gaviotas Country Club couldn't seat the extras and still comply with fire code regulations.

And there were more than a half dozen letters from former players, including a Navy engineer, a college administrator and local pastor, who wanted to be there, but couldn't.

"I love these kids," said O'Brien. "This did me good."

The players said it did them good, too.

"What people really talked about was how we were always ready to play," said William "Fella" Rhodes, 54, Class of 64 and associate broker for William E. Wood and Associates. "He taught us values that you carried with you for life.

"It wasn't enough to win. We had to win right."

There was no taunting, no cheap fouls, Rhodes said. Even star players rode the bench if they stepped out of line, he said.

In his three years of varsity ball from 1961 to 1963, Kenny Barefoot said Great Bridge lost only once, but wasn't always the most athletic team.

O'Brien found a way to win and convinced his teams they could win, Barefoot said. He cared who his players hung out with, he made sure their class work was done, Barefoot said.

Barefoot went on to play football at Virginia Tech, then to the National Football League, where he played for the Washington Redskins and Coach Vince Lombardi.

O'Brien "taught me more about football and life than anybody," said Barefoot, Class of '64 and the manager of the William E. Wood office where Rhodes works.

State Del. Harry B. Blevins, R-Chesapeake, who coached with O'Brien for nine years from the late 1950s to the mid 1960s, said players recalled summer training camp at Camp Farrar, a former 4-H camp, in Virginia Beach.

O'Brien started the tradition after a star underclassman, Billy Dunbar, was struck and killed by a truck while walking to summer practice.

That wouldn't happen again, O'Brien told Blevins.

For the next 15 years, O'Brien took his players to camp, so that he could keep a close eye on them. It was boot camp. There were bed inspections and a regimented schedules. His teams bonded.

And in 2002, the players will come together again. The reunion organizers intend to have get-togethers for O'Brien-led teams every other year.

"They're already talking about the next one," O'Brien said.

Coaching Excellence
The stuff of legends

It was a couple years after graduating from Great Bridge High School in 1961. Far off in Gainesville, Florida, I sat with my teammates at a banquet honoring the University of Florida's victory over Penn State in the 1992 Gator Bowl game. The speaker was Shug Jordan, widely respected and beloved coach of the Auburn Tigers football team.

He talked of the admirable work of my college coach, Ray Graves, his staff and of coaching excellence in general. And he told a story of a particularly exemplary bit of coaching.

It happened during the shot-put finals at the Virginia state track and field championship a year or so earlier, he said. "One of the favorites, a long, sturdy youngster stepped in the circle for his first throw. The result was awful—49 feet and change, far off the distance necessary to win. The young fellow walked off dejected, tugging at the fingers on his throwing hand. As the next contestant readied himself to throw, the first youngster's coach came over, put his arm around the boy and quietly and earnestly whispered some words of instruction.

"Clearly," Jordan continued, "those words were well-chosen. For the next time the young man stepped into the circle, he exploded out of a tight crouch and launched the shot-put far beyond anyone's reach that day, far beyond the state record. Yes, that was coaching at its very best," Shug Jordan allowed.

The story was eerily familiar to me. Afterwards, I approached Coach Jordan and asked the origin of his tale. He had heard it from his close friend, Jerry Claibourne, new head coach of VPI in Blacksburg, Virginia, Jordan replied. "Coach Claibourne was there that day, recruiting a kid for his football team," he added.

I was startled. I was that kid. I was that shot-putter. Coach Claibourne had been recruiting me for some time and was there in the gallery the day of the shot-put

1

finals. And that coach, that insightful tactician with just the right words of wisdom for his young shot-putter, was none other than Billy O'Brien.

I filled in "the rest of the story" for Coach Jordan, and we both marveled at the coincidence. After a bit of banter, Coach Jordan leaned close to me and quite earnestly asked, "Son, what exactly did your coach say to you that day?" I shrugged and said that he—Coach Jordan—pretty much had it right. Bill O'Brien just knew what to say and when to say it.

I just couldn't bring myself to tell him what really transpired the day of the shot-put finals.

With that first throw, the ball had slipped from my hand, snapping my index finger backwards painfully. I stepped out of the circle, massaging the finger to get the feeling back in it. Coach O'Brien rushed over, put his arm around my shoulder and said, "Jeez, Johnny, you OK?" Assured that I was, he then said, "OK, OK… Look, just… just throw it out there. You know, get under it… and just throw it." Then he turned and walked nervously to the gallery to watch my next throw.

On my second time into the circle, I just "threw it out there," just as coach had told me.

The moral of the story? In the making of a coaching legend, it's rarely the brilliance of anything spoken at a critical time. Rather, it's all that went before: all the hours employed in developing talent, all the persistence, all the repetition, all the head games, all the prodding, pushing and, yes, agitating. It's not easy to get the best out of half-boy/half-man.

In that small episode at a long-forgotten track meet 40 years ago, that young shot-putter didn't excel for a fleeting moment because some larger-than-life coach had just the right words to say at the right time. The youngster performed because that coach, in his own distinctive way, kindled and stoked a fire in his student over four years, a fire to test the fullest extent of his capabilities. What a marvelous gift to bestow upon a person.

From an old Bill O'Brien--coached shot-putter/wrestler/football player, I extend heartfelt thanks to the person who dragged the man out of the boy that was me.

Johnny Thompson
Great Bridge High School
Class of 1961

Allen Hall
206 Pond View Lane
Fort Mill, South Carolina 29715
803-547-6195

Hello Coach,

Thought I'd drop you a line every 20 years or so, just for general principal.

The MRI of my spine looks like a used po-go stick. Spurs on most vertebra and a whopper of a ruptured disc between Cervicle 6/7. So thanks for running me a million times in 1965. Especially the game, don't remember which one, you called my "Hall knock right/left" 52 times. It may still be a Va. HS record.

That was one of Dad's favorite stories. You may remember he met with you and complained that Allen would run the ball all the way to red zone, then other plays were called. Next game you showed Frank, wham-mo, 52 carries. I heard him tell that story, one more time, not long before he passed on 12-19-94. I guess it really made an impression on him.....for the story to last 30+ years.

How are you and Joyce? Hope all of you are doing great. The grape vine told me you coached again somewhere. I always figured you would end up as a major college or pro head coach, you always had the "right stuff". Too bad we (you) didn't win the (close) run for the House, we might have been in DC now to witness the most screwed up political mess in history. On second thought, perhaps it all worked out for the best.

For what it's worth, thanks for being a football coach/teacher. Your guidance and leadership made a real difference in my life. I never stopped running the "Hall Knock Right" and it has served me well. All those lessons you taught in football carried over into life, just as you said they would..... way back in the '60's. It's uncanny how life can be capsulized into four quarters of a football game. As corny and overused as it is, it's true.

To learn and experience (at an early age) that you can still win, even in the last minute of the 4th quarter, is very important. Learning to win and lose with dignity and humility with an eye on the "next game" is crucial to lasting success and happiness. Tenacity, honor, dignity, self reliance/confidence, compassion, ethics, and trust (to name a few) are all products of your quality football program. These things dwarf the score of any actual contest. Congratulations.

I can't help thinking how lucky we all were to have experienced the '60's together. Looking back is not one of my strong points, I usually keep blinders on to point me only forward. But things are so much different now, to say the least. We had trust, discipline and order then, except for my one slip with the chair throwing episode. OK, I'll now admit it.... was.... Danny Carpenters idea. Ho, ho...You believe me, don't you? You really saved my butt on that one.

To prove I'm still running a "Knock Right", I've enclosed a picture of my 6.5 year old daughter Meagan Lindsay. Nancee and I are having a lot of fun with her. (Wait a minute, I'm only 52.)

As they say, if you're ever in the Charlotte area........! I'm the CEO of CWD which owns and operates FCC mobile comm. license's in NC/SC area. It's a private channel business fleet two-way radio company. I've been in the mobile communications field since the late 70's.

Perhaps this is the most unexpected communication you've received lately. I just decided to act on some long overdue thoughts, now that I'm in the middle of the "3rd quarter".

Have a great Christmas and successful 1999.

Best Personal Regards,

"Knock Right" Hall
pirate23@aol.com

ALLEN HALL
President

Carolina Wireless Dispatch, Inc.

415 Minuet Lane • Suite E • Charlotte, North Carolina 28217
NC 704-527-2322 • Fax 704-527-2212 • Pager 704-565-4438

10/9/00

Coach + Mrs. O'Brien,

Enclosed please find my check for the evening Saturday night. I forgot to give it to you before I left.

Thank you so much for allowing me to relive so many great memories on Saturday. From the time I was 8 or 9 years old I hoped to be able to wear the green + gold + be a Wildcat. Actually being able to do it was truly one of the great times in my life. For many years, G-B

-2-

football was a big part of the Head family's life. I have always been sorry that my younger brother Cam didn't get the chance to be a part of it. Indian River just didn't measure up!!

Since I am still in coaching I couldn't help but think about all the talent that was there Saturday. The list of running backs was incredible Pratt, Royster, McManus, Roberson, Crisswell, + Hinton. I'd love to have just one of them right now!! Of course, my all time favorite was a little guy named Wayne.

-3-

Thanks again for your efforts in planning such a great week-end. I only hope that I can make the same impact on my players that the coaches of GBHS made on me. I know I am in coaching today because of the role models that influenced me.

I hope that the week-end was as special for you as it was for me. Thanks for everything,

Love,
Mike Head

Sept. 20, 2000

Dear Coach —

It is with great sadness that I write this letter. I will be unable to attend the reunion in October. I picked up the option to extend my contract with the tour of Beauty and the Beast. I requested my vacation for the dates that would include the reunion dates but unfortunately, due to other contracted obligations for time off, my request was denied.

I sincerely hope that the reunion is a smashing success, as I am sure it will be. This is a wonderful thing you're doing. I know the number of young people that you have influenced over the years appreciate your endeavor. Please extend my best to all of those that I shared the "Wildcat" experience with both as classmates and teacher.

All the best to you and Joyce, and please extend the same to Joey —

With lots of love to one
Hell of a guy

Ron Lee Savin A/K/A

Ronnie Lee

TRAVEL ADDRESS
RON LEE SAVIN
C/o Beauty + the Beast Tour
1450 Broadway, 3rd fl
NY, NY 10018
Cell Phone (917)570-7431

DONALD C. WILLIAMS
12107 GORDON SCHOOL ROAD
RICHMOND, VIRGINIA 23236

The Honorable J. W. "Billy" O'Brien
1156 Pond Cypress Drive
Virginia Beach, Virginia 23455

Dear Coach O'Brien:

Last month, albeit on the sad occasion of Stanley's funeral, it was good to see you, the team and coaches from those long ago days of Wildcat Football.

I am excited about the prospect of joining you and 20 years worth of Wildcats on October 6 and 7. It sounds like a good time will be had by all – reacquainting ourselves with one another and finding out just what we have been up to over all these years.

Enclosed is my reply and personal check for the weekend's activities. As you can see I plan on attending the Bar-B-Que and game on Friday night with my family. I hope that families can be accommodated; if not, please let me know. Also, on Saturday I am planning to have a foursome play golf – some of my associates here in Richmond have heard so much about being one of Billy O'Brien's boys that they are interested in experiencing what it is like to be a Wildcat. Then, my wife and I plan on attending the dinner on Saturday night.

In addition, I am enclosing a check from Murray Farms LLC, in the amount of $100.00. This is a donation from my brother B.M. (Class of '68) and me. In talking with Curtis Hall, he suggested that sponsorship money could be used and that recognition at the golf outing would be in order. Let me know if you need additional information for the sponsorship program.

In closing, I would also note that B.M. has yet to receive any information about the weekend. I would recommend that someone call him at 482-4321, or write at 1201 Murray Drive, Chesapeake, VA 23322.

I look forward to an exciting and memorable weekend.

Sincerely,

Donald C. Williams
Class of 1972
Wildcat Number "72"

Edwin L. Baker III, M.D.

205 Londonderry Drive
Lumberton, NC 28358

Phone (910) 738-2454
Home Phone (910) 738-8344
Email baker@carolina.

Dear Coach,

It was a pleasant moment in an otherwise intense day in the operating room to receive your letter regarding the Wildcat reunion in early October.

I am chagrined that I will have to miss it due to an obligation at a medical meeting out of the country, but, I will be there in spirit.

My time as a Wildcat gave me a good start toward dealing with the challenges of this life: whether it was the "Ratline" at VMI, the gruelling pace of UVa medical school or my struggles in the Desert of Iraq as a FAST team surgeon during Operation Desert Storm.

My time as a Wildcat was a wonderful gift in my life and I'm sorry I'll miss a reunion I'd love to be at. Take care of yourself and enjoy all the much deserved praise you receive.

Sincerely,

Ed Bak

Edwin Baker #24
1975-1976

P.S. Tell coach Calhoun to take a lap and Kent Eley, Donald Lane and Tim Spruill to give me 10 pushups!!

Feb. 8, 2002

Dear Coach O'Brien:

It struck me today that I never wrote you back to thank you for the nice letter you sent after our Deep Creek game!

It was such an honor to have you in attendance that night!! To see you come walking out on the field during pre-game brought me to tears. It was 1966 again and we were getting ready to play.

It's no accident that you saw many things during the game that reminded you of the old wildcats. Your "preaching" did not fall on deaf ears. Many of the subtleties that you built our success on back then, I have tried to incorporate into our program over the years. Your influence on me was immeasurable! I appreciate all that you did for this skinny kid. I cherish the memories of playing for you.

Please come again! I'd love to have you speak to our players before a game next year.

My best,

Lew(is)

Michael J. Caddy
24660 Paradise Lane
Hollywood, MD 20636

Dear Mr. O'Brien

Thank you for the invitations to homecoming. I am very sorry that I will not be able to come. The last one I attended I hardly recognized any of the old class members. You may not remember me but you sure left an impression on me. I was in the class of 1961, number 38, played left tackle. At this time in my development I stuttered badly. I guess for this reason I was not in the social click of that age. For this reason I never really developed a social connection outside of the sports. I thank you to the discipline and for the influences that you instilled in me as coach. After high school I lost all contact with any of the team and went on my way. At the last homecoming no one really spoke to me or to my wife.

For the record: I went on to Virginia Tech into engineering. In 1964 I married a Radford graduate that went to Virginia Beach High School. We met in college and did not know each other until college. In 1965 I graduated in Aerospace Engineering. In 1961 there were 265 freshmen in the class. I was very tough. While most left the curriculum, some dropped out. In 1965 when I graduated there were only 6 of us left. I was number 3. I never played college ball although i was offered a position. I was afraid that my knee would blow out again. I went to work for the Navy in Pennsylvania. In 1972 I received Masters Degree in Aerospace Engineering at Drexel University.

Today I am still working for the Naval Air System Command in Maryland. I am the senior performance engineer responsible for the aircraft catapult performance analysis relating to the Joint Strike Fighter, JSF. This will be the largest fighter procurement in the history of the Department of Defense. In this capacity I am the best of the best in aircraft simulation in this technical expert field. I have one U. S. Government Patent and numerous awards. I have been an invitational guess lecturer at several universities. Currently I am teaching part time for Johns Hopkins University. My wife and I enjoy the Maryland life style and water adventures.

My wife provided me with 2 wonderful daughters. Understanding the value and necessity of sports I made sure my daughters were fully involved through out high school. We were very lucky to have two very intelligent girls. Our first one Andrea was very athletic in high school, lettering in swimming, track, tennis and basketball. In her senior year she was captain of track, tennis and basketball. When she graduated she held 34 letters, which at that time was a school record. After high school she went to the Air Force Academy and graduated in 1988 as an Aerospace Engineer. At graduation she married another graduate and now lives in Texas. She became a pilot and graduated first in her class. Because of her pilot skills she became an instructor pilot for the T-38 jet. After seven years in the Air Force she left and became a pilot for Northwest Airlines flying a DC-9. She also still flying in the Air Force reserved as a C-5A commander pilot. I have 2 wonderful grandchildren.

My other daughter Cheri also was exceptional. She skipped the 3 grade went though high school not quite as athletic as her sister but more the student. She graduated and went to Norwich University in Vermont. Because of her academic record in high school she tested out of a lot of college courses and graduated from a 4-year college at the age of 19. She later went on to get masters from the University of Virginia in foreign affairs. Now she works for the Federal Government for the Food and Drug Administration.

Coach O'Brien, life has been wonderful to me. I am both healthy and happy. I again thank you for the influence and structure that you added to my teenage development.

I doubt if any one will ask about me at the reunion. Please feel free to share this letter with anyone who does.

Respectfully,

M J Caddy

Michael Caddy, Class of 1961, #38

GREAT HOPE BAPTIST CHURCH

1401 S. Battlefield Blvd.
Chesapeake, VA 23322
Phone: (757) 482-1177 / Fax: (757) 546-0699

John W. Godfrey, Pastor

Dear Coach,

Thank you for the invitation to reunite with the best men who wore the green and gold. I may be the only Baptist preacher in the group for this celebration, but I am excited about seeing some of the fellows I was privileged to play with.

Coach you were a much better football strategist than a legislator. I am going to over look your weakness in giving us the lottery in Virginia, and try to make the last Quarter of the game.
The sixties were the height of Great Bridge football, and it was because Billy O'Brien was the brain on the sidelines. There were few if any that could whip a team into winning form like Bulldog O'Brien.

Coach I have never made this known but I was obsessed with the goal of coaching football. My total reason for going to college was to one-day coach. I never had great natural speed or abilities accept maybe a pair of good hands, and a hard head   the one thing that football gave me was that I had to work for what I got.. Through contact with a little baseball player at Ferrum Jr. College and a concerned Christian family I eventually came to know Jesus Christ personally. Needless to say my world was turned up side down, and direction for life changed. God has graciously used our lives in lifetime ministry for the last 28 years. God has allowed us to start a Christian high school. And another Christian school from scratch, with 23 of these years spent in the pastorate.
  The stakes to win get bigger as life moves on. The scoreboard at the ball game gets turned off, but the real game of life never ends. I don't know how my football experience helps me in the ministry today, but it didn't make me a looser. The sober truth is that I still toss and turn some nights as I try to fix the few games we lost under your leadership. They cannot be revisited or altered and will have little or no impact on our lives. Coach, thanks for teaching us to win! There is no substitute for a winning spirit. There is too much at stake here at Great Hope Baptist church and school for us to bow to defeat.
I can't make the barbecue because of a wedding, but will make part of the game .

Because of His Grace

Pastor John W. Godfrey

My name is Bob Royster, class of 1960. I had the good fortune of playing for coach O'Brien in the seasons of 1956, '57, '58 and '59.

Some of the happiest days of my life were the years I played for Coach O'Brien. To this day, I think he was the best high school coach that ever coached in this area. He was more than a coach; he was a mentor and also a father figure to me. I still think of him fondly after all these years, and I am grateful for all that he did for me.

I know this is not a roast of Coach O'Brien but I must tell this short story. My earliest and fondest memory of Coach O'Brien occurred in the fall of 1956 when I had coach O'Brien as my health class teacher. About halfway through the lecture, I looked up and Coach O'Brien had slid down in his seat, and I could barely see the top of his head. His long legs were draped across the side of the desk and his feet dangled over the edge. He was lecturing from the textbook. Guess the topic of the lecture. You guessed it— proper sitting posture! The memory of that moment is still very clear in my mind; I can't help but chuckle about it.

If anyone ever doubted if Coach O'Brien loved his players, this terrible story will erase those doubts. On August 28, 1959, we were just starting morning practice for our season opener with Princess Anne. I was one of the team captains and we had started doing calisthenics but the coaches had not arrived. Suddenly I turned around and looked about 20 yards behind me. Coach O'Brien was talking to Coach Calhoun and Coach Blevins. In a flash, Coach O'Brien spun away from the 2 coaches and flung himself to the ground. He screamed out loud as he rolled and beat his fists on the ground. This went on for several minutes. Not knowing what had happened and not knowing what to do, I told the team to take a knee. I ran over to Coach Calhoun and he told me that a truck had killed one of our teammates as he walked to practice that morning. His name was Billy Dunbar. Billy was only a sophomore, but he had a good chance of becoming a starter that year, and I am positive that Billy would have been Coach O'Brien's first All-State track star. This tragedy stunned everyone, but we all knew that Billy would want us to carry on. Despite his obvious heartbreak and anguish, Coach O'Brien managed to gather himself and prepare the team for our upcoming game. In front of 10,000 screaming fans at PA's stadium, the Wildcats went on to defeat them 6–0 for our first-ever win over PA. I will always remember Billy Dunbar as a great person and his almost limitless potential as an athlete. I am sure Coach O'Brien feels that same way.

Memories of Coach O'Brien & Coach Calhoun and the Wildcats

I am writing this on behalf of Stan Lancaster, Jr., our son, who deceased August 13, 2000. From what we hold in our memories, we can recall so many wonderful moments at the Great Bridge High School Stadium and being a part of Coach O'Brien's and Coach Calhoun's team.

We recall that Coach O'Brien was a very innovative coach. He was willing to take chances for that BIG win and boy did we win BIG. Great Bridge High had a BIG name that all other area schools knew.

Coach O'Brien also knew how to bring out the best in players like Ken Barefoot, Fella Rhodes, Lora Hinton, our son, Stan and all the other team members. He knew how to optimize each one's potential. He gave them confidence, leadership and allowed them to play at their fullest capacity. He taught teamwork. Each guy knew that without those other guys supporting each position, that their job would not come as easy.

Coach O'Brien was creative with football. That made football more interesting for the guys on the field who practiced for hours and hours but especially to us in the stands. We remember one game when Stan made a touchdown reception as his body was fully extended, one of those Kodak moments, however Coach O'Brien had surprised the opposing team by having him receive the ball instead of passing the ball in his normal position of quarterback. We also recall a drive at the 1 foot yard line where Troy Anchors played quarterback to make that winning touchdown drive when his normal position was lineman. As you can see, Coach O'Brien taught his players to seize the opportunity and to be an unselfish team member.

Coach O'Brien and Coach Calhoun were also practical jokers. Stan came to practice late one time and both coaches would not ever let him live it down since being at practice on time was highest priority in their coaching book.

The coaches were also organized in football and school as well. This helped students and football players to be more well rounded.

In closing, we would like to mention that Coach O'Brien and Coach Calhoun stayed in touch with their players. In return each player loved and respected both coaches.

During the past several months Stan had spoke to us many times about this event and how much he looked forward to this reunion. We can truly say that Stan loved playing football at Great Bridge High and he loved being a part of Coach O'Brien's and Coach Calhoun's team. We know that it was this team & the coaches' leadership that put Great Bridge on the map. Thank you coaches and GO WILDCATS!!!!

Stanley & Glenna Lancaster